ORGANIZATIONAL BEHAVIOR: MANAGING AND LEADING ORGANIZATIONS

ORGANIZATIONAL BEHAVIOR: MANAGING AND LEADING ORGANIZATIONS

Belal A. Kaifi

Breezeway Books

ISBN: 978-1-62550-608-5

Published in the United States of America

DEDICATION

This book is dedicated to students, researchers, and practitioners who strive to understand and improve contemporary organizations.

ACKNOWLEDGEMENTS

Many people have contributed directly or indirectly to the preparation of this book. Students in various classes that I have taught have provided me with the inspiration and feedback that helped shape the organization and the content of the book. Discussions with colleagues and graduate students have helped sharpen my thinking. To all of those people, I say thank you. I thank my editors and reviewers (Wajma Aslami, Lisa Jensen Cook, Layma Murtaza, Ahmad Kaifi, Milaly Kaifi, Maryam Kaifi, Karen Hesse, Lois Hammond, and Yalda Tarin) who gave me many wonderful suggestions. I would like to thank Dr. Jason A. Colquitt for being an outstanding professor. Finally, I thank my family for all of their love and support.

TABLE OF CONTENTS

PREFACE

Organizational behavior is a broad field that uses concepts from a number of disciplines to help explain why the people in organizations behave the way they do. For centuries, scholars and researchers from diverse backgrounds and disciplines have discussed important organizational behavior topics. Each chapter of this book provides valuable information for current (and future) managers and leaders. By understanding and embracing the concepts in this book, managers and leaders will become more effective when dealing with organizational behavior issues. Additionally, students in college should be required to take an organizational behavior course before graduating and entering the demanding and frustrating workforce.

Chapter 1 introduces the contributions of early organizational behavior researchers and several fundamental organizational behavior constructs that have a number of managerial implications. This chapter also addresses how organizational behavior is a unique field that is connected to a number of disciplines. Chapter 2 discusses the importance of human resources in organizations. In addition, non-traditional performance strategies are addressed for managers and leaders to take into consideration. Chapter 3 discusses the importance of effective organizational leadership. For example, different leadership styles can be used for enhancing productivity levels. This chapter also addresses the different traits that experienced leaders possess and the lifecycle of leadership development. Chapter 4 discusses the relationship between job performance and citizenship behaviors in the workforce. This chapter also addresses counterproductive behaviors in the workforce. Several performance management tools that can be used for assessing performance are also highlighted in this chapter. Chapter 5 discusses organizational commitment and includes an organizational commitment survey. This chapter addresses the different models that have been used to understand organizational commitment. Chapter 6 discusses job satisfaction and the different work values that influence job satisfaction. A survey related to job satisfaction is also highlighted. Professions that typically have high levels of job satisfaction are addressed. Chapter 7 discusses a number of motivational theories. This chapter also addresses the importance of using non-cash incentives to motivate employees. Chapter 8 discusses organizational culture and the organizational culture profile. Furthermore, this chapter underscores the organizational cultures of two commendable organizations. A number of examples are used to help illustrate key points. Chapter 9 provides ten exclusive interviews with managers from different generations. Each manager has a unique philosophy on organizational issues. The interviewees also provide valuable knowledge for future leaders and managers based upon their vast experiences. Finally, Chapter 10 discusses the future of organizations and the challenges that managers and leaders will face. For example, managers and leaders will have to focus on a multi-generational workforce, the use of teams, and gender equality in the workforce. This chapter also addresses the importance of managers and leaders developing new skills in order to be effective.

Moreover, each theoretical chapter is equipped with chapter review questions, discussion questions, a case study, case study questions, and a special case assignment. The purpose of this book is to provide indispensable organizational behavior concepts in a straightforward, practical, and concise manner. I hope that you benefit from reading this book.

~ Belal A. Kaifi

"Choose a job you love, and you will never have to work a day in your life."

~ Confucius

"If I had eight hours to chop down a tree, I'd spend six sharpening my ax."

~ Abraham Lincoln

"Whatever your life's work is, do it well. A man should do his job so well that the living, the dead, and the unborn could do it no better."

~ Martin Luther King Jr.

"One machine can do the work of fifty ordinary men. No machine can do the work of one extraordinary man."

~ Elbert Hubbard

1

Introduction to Organizational Behavior

With thousands of people entering the workforce each year, it becomes imperative for students, practitioners, and researchers to learn more about the people working in organizations and how they function in a controlled environment. A classic example of how people function in organizations is highlighted in the film, *Modern Times* (1936). The movie portrays Charlie Chaplin as a factory worker employed on an assembly line. After experiencing a number of indignities, he suffers a nervous breakdown resulting in many organizational dilemmas. Organizational behavior (OB) is a field of study devoted to recognizing, evaluating, and developing the attitudes and behaviors of people (individuals and groups) within organizations. It is based on scientific knowledge and applied practice. According to Kaifi (2011), the "RED Analysis" can be applied by professionals, practitioners, and researchers for decision-making purposes as well as for understanding organizational issues. Diagnosing organizational behavior is an ongoing cycle of recognizing the main problem, evaluating and critically analyzing the main problem, and continuously developing action plans, best practices, and strategies that can help an organization transform into a robust, high-performing, and dynamic entity. As an example, the RED Analysis can be used by an interviewee during a behavioral-based interview. An HR recruiter may ask a prospective manager the following question: Have you had to convince a team to work on a project they weren't thrilled about? How did you do it? It is imperative for the interviewee to be able to recognize the problem, evaluate the problem, and then develop an action plan for how the situation can be resolved. This step-by-step process allows an individual to systematically diagnose and treat the problem (as can be seen in Figure 1).

RED Analysis
Figure 1

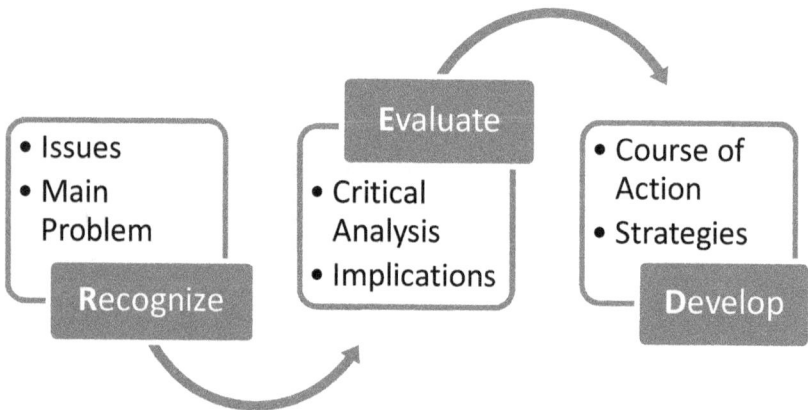

It must be mentioned that organizations need strong managers who are capable of planning, organizing, leading, and controlling an organization. Leaders who understand both management and human resource management have a competitive advantage because they are able to influence specific behaviors that help shape the culture of an organization. Influencing specific behaviors in an organization can be a difficult task to undertake for a number of reasons. The most obvious reason is that humans are unpredictable and have unique attitudes and perspectives. When people enter the workforce, they also bring their expectations and experiences with them, which may not correlate with the organization's values. This creates an immediate dilemma that can be contagious to others (i.e., emotional contagion theory). Controlling such organizational problems can be a battle with no end, which accurately explains *why* the study of organizational behavior is so important. Being able to diagnose organizational behavior issues and respond with well-formulated solutions is what many organizational behavior researchers and managers strive to accomplish. The two primary outcomes of organizational behavior are job performance and organizational commitment (Colquitt, Lepine, & Wesson, 2011, p. 8).

Although organizational behavior is an applied discipline, students are not "trained in organizational behavior. Rather, they are educated in organizational behavior and are a co-producer in learning" (Nelson & Quick, 2011, p. 25). The study of organizational behavior requires a rudimentary understanding of psychology, anthropology, sociology, philosophy, and axiology. From a psychological perspective, human behaviors and mental processes dictate how the people in organizations perform. An anthropological perspective demonstrates that the culture, values, and beliefs of an individual dictate how an organization and coworkers (i.e., subordinates and managers) are regarded. From a sociological perspective, the development of social behavior dictates how the people in organizations work collectively to complete tasks; while a philosophical perspective proposes that the morals and ethics of an individual dictate how an organization's rules and regulations are interpreted. Finally, an axiological perspective suggests that an individual's values dictate feelings of satisfaction and commitment. Other disciplines (e.g., economics, engineering, and social psychology) have historically also been applied to organizational behavior. For example, in 1776 Adam Smith published *The Wealth of Nations*, in which he explained the economic advantages of "division of labor" (breakdown of jobs into narrow and repetitive tasks) in organizations. This diversity in organizational behavior allows researchers to investigate new avenues for dealing with organizational behavior issues from different perspectives and angles.

Early OB Researchers

Many organizational behavior researchers dating back to the 1800s understood that organizations need to put "people first" because they are an organization's most important asset. More specifically, five OB researchers revolutionized this notion of organizations putting people first for achieving optimum results: Robert Owen and Andrew Ure (both during the early1800s), Hugo Munsterberg and Mary Parker Follett (in the early 1900s), and Chester Barnard (during the 1930s). In the 19th century, Robert Owen, who was a social-reformer from England, came up with a novel idea (a.k.a. Owenism) related to organizational behavior. He realized that if workers were treated better, productivity levels would rise, and as a result, profits would also rise. In 1835, Andrew Ure from England published a book, *The Philosophy of Manufacturers*, within which he was able to underscore the importance of workers being treated better by receiving medical treatment, access to water or hot tea on a regular basis, good ventilation, and even sick leave—all of which have become the norm in most industrialized nations. Hugo Munsterberg created the field of industrial psychology—scientific study of people at work. He suggested the usage of psychological tests to better understand employee motivation and behavior. In the early years of the 20th century, Mary Parker Follett, a political and business philosopher, was able to highlight three important concepts that were all ahead of her time. She stated that (1) workers should be involved in the decision making process, (2) the workplace is dynamic and needs to constantly change in order to be able to compete with its competitors, and (3) that humanizing the workforce can help with recruitment and retention. In addition, Mary Parker Follett also introduced the concepts of "conflict resolution, authority and power, and the task of leadership—she approached management through human values" (Samuel, 1996, p. 865). Chester Barnard published *The Functions of the Executive* (1938) and was the "first to argue that organizations are open systems" (Robbins & Coulter, 2005, p. 33). Open systems dynamically interact with their environment. In contrast, closed systems are not influenced by and do not interact with their environment. It should be mentioned that closed systems are becoming rare. Some examples of closed system organizations are the regional armies of the People's Republic of China (Shambaugh, 1991); spiritual cults (e.g., Waco); Camp X-Ray in Guantanamo Bay; and prison systems (Fong, Vogel, & Buentello, 1995). With globalization, technological advancements, and unlimited competition, organizations are more likely to become open systems and interact extensively with their environment. Lastly, Chester Barnard was able to realize the correlation between effective communication by a manager and higher performance levels of workers.

The Four P's of Organizations

In the field of organizational behavior, it is important to understand the Four P's (purpose, people, plan, and priorities) of organizations. Organizations have a *purpose* for existing, employ *people* who have specific skills and traits, have a *plan* for producing and becoming successful, and have *priorities* that need to be accomplished in a timely manner. According to Schwartz, Jones, and McCarty (2010), "No matter how much value we produce today—whether it's measured in dollars or sales or goods or widgets—it's never enough" (p. 3). The Four P's to understanding organizations as systems (Kaifi, 2010; Kaifi & Noori, 2011, p. 90) is depicted in Figure 2:

The Four P's of Organizations
Figure 2

Hawthorne Experiments

In the late 1920s, a group of scientific management scholars from Harvard University went to Hawthorne, Illinois to study the effects of physical factors (e.g., light) on workers and their productivity. More specifically, Elton Mayo, (the driving force behind the Hawthorne studies) and his colleagues spent five years studying workers, productivity levels, and physical factors. As a result of these studies, Mayo was able to report two important discoveries related to organizational behavior. First, workers perform at higher levels when they are being watched by a superior, and second, workers perform at higher levels when they are a part of a team. The implications of these studies and the research of other early researchers have influenced contemporary organizations in a number of ways. For example, modern organizations are notorious for having supervisors at every level. In the corporate world, there are first line managers, middle managers, and top managers. Many organizations, such as police departments, are highly structured with a number of leaders who hold different ranks (e.g., sergeant, lieutenant, captain, chief, etc.). Such highly structured organizations can create a political climate that can either positively or negatively influence organizational behavior. As a result of Mayo's second finding, organizations use teams in many situations. An example is hospitals, which have a number of teams within each department. These teams work collectively and must perform at very high levels because people's lives are literally on the line. This same philosophy is true in organized sports. When playing on a sports team, one is more inclined to perform at higher levels because of the influence by the entire team and not wanting to let his or her team down. Pfeffer and Veiga (1999) explained how teams can be successful, "Implementing work teams will not accomplish much, unless the teams receive training in specific technical skills and team processes, and are given financial and operating performance goals and information" (p. 47). As a result, organizations have embraced the team approach for most situations.

The field of organizational behavior is growing rapidly and will continue to grow because of its implication on modern organizations. This chapter illuminated the importance of employees being the most important asset of an organization and that if they are managed correctly, they will be much more productive, efficient, and effective. Interestingly enough, the rule of one-eighth as described by Pfeffer and Veiga (1999) explains:

> One must bear in mind that one-half of organizations won't believe the connection between how they manage their people and the profits they earn. One-half of those who do see the connection will do what many organizations have done—try to make a single change to solve their problems, not realizing that the effective management of people requires a more comprehensive and systematic approach. Of the firms that make comprehensive changes, probably only about one-half will persist with their practices long enough to actually drive economic benefits. Since one-half times one-half times one-half equals one-eighth, at best 12 percent of organizations will actually do what is required to build profits *by putting people first* (p. 47).

The Rule of One-Eighth
Figure 3

$$(½) \times (½) \times (½) = ⅛ \approx 12\%$$

The importance of putting people first in organizations cannot be stressed enough for a number of reasons that will be discussed throughout this book. Unfortunately, only 12 percent of organizations have embraced this notion of putting people (i.e., employees) first. Google is an organization that consistently ranks among the best companies at which to work. They have implemented strategies that have helped with recruitment and retention of employees. Google has a reputation for spoiling their employees and reaping the much wanted benefits such as employee loyalty, productivity, synergy, and unity. Schwartz, Jones, & McCarty (2010) state, "No company we've encountered comes close to the kind of investment Google makes in feeding its employees or treats food as a more integral part of its overall culture" (p. 118). Google has been able to think outside of the box by finding unique strategies to boost performance levels. For example, at Google, healthy meals and snacks are all free for employees. Schwartz, Jones, & McCarty (2010) continue to explain, "At Google, there is just a single vending machine on its main campus, and it's there to make a point" and further states, "The machine is filled with candy and other junk food, but items are priced in inverse proportion to their nutritional value. The worst foods cost the most" (p. 117-118). At its Mountain View headquarters, Google has several different (free) restaurants for employees to have lunch. Google has many other resources available to their employees that make the organization an outstanding place for employment. Beyond the basics of generous pay, benefits, and time to work on their own projects, Google tries to anticipate its employees' needs to save them from wasting time on personal distractions. As a result, medical care, gourmet cafeterias, child care, gym, lap pool, language classes, self-service laundry, and shuttle bus service are all available on site and for free (Bolman & Deal, 2008, p. 139). More importantly, Google has embraced the concept of "Owenism"—if employees are treated better, productivity levels will rise, and as a result, profits will rise.

Summary

Chapter 1 introduced the contributions of early organizational behavior researchers and several fundamental organizational behavior constructs that have a number of managerial implications. This chapter also addressed how organizational behavior is a unique field that is connected to a number of disciplines. In addition, a number of examples were used to help illustrate key points.

Chapter Review Questions

1. Define organizational behavior. What is its focus?

2. What are the two primary outcomes of organizational behavior?

3. What is "Owenism" and where did it originate?

4. What are the Four P's in relation to understanding organizations?

5. What is the RED Analysis?

6. What was discovered in the Hawthorne studies?

7. How did Mary Parker Follet influence the field of organizational behavior?

8. What is the Rule of One-Eighth? Do you agree with the rule?

9. Why does Google consistently rank among the best organizations to work for?

10. How does organizational behavior relate to anthropology, philosophy, and psychology?

Discussion Questions

1. Why is the study of organizational behavior imperative?

2. What factors influence organizational behavior?

3. Discuss two ways that people learn about organizational behavior.

Case Study

XYZ Radiology is a company that analyzes digital images for major hospitals in Florida. The company has a total of five seasoned radiologists who specialize in analyzing routine digital images, CT scans, MRI's, and Mammograms. Hospitals throughout Florida outsource their digital images to *XYZ Radiology* because of their reputation for quick turn-around times and keen skills of evaluating difficult cases. Michael Logan, the CEO of the company spends one day a week at *XYZ Radiology* dealing with potential clients. Logan has a reputation for exploiting his workers. He recently heard from a "good source" that productivity levels have been fluctuating at *XYZ Radiology* and that several of the radiologists are doing "less work" or purposely seeking the "easier exams" to analyze. He is stumped and calls his friend who is an "organizational development doctor" to analyze and diagnose his company's ailments.

Case Questions

1. What questions would the organizational development doctor ask Michael Logan?

2. What questions would the organizational development doctor ask the radiologists?

3. Based on the case, who is at fault? Explain why.

4. Conduct a RED Analysis on this case and explain your findings.

5. How can the work of Robert Owen, Andrew Ure, and Elton Mayo be applied to this case?

Special Case Assignment

Suppose that Michael Logan went home that evening and created a short survey to hand out to each radiologist the following morning. His goal is to make things "better" in his company.

Create a 10-question survey with a 5-point scale for each question (ranging from strongly disagree to strongly agree) relating to teamwork that could be used to yield important data for Michael Logan.

2

ORGANIZATIONS

As organizations evolve, the human resources of the establishment are expected to be more efficient, effective, and productive. *The Way We're Working Isn't Working* by authors Schwartz, Jones, and McCarthy (2010) succinctly addresses organizational behavior, development, and change. The authors are quick to point out that organizations are dynamic and must be able to compete in this global 24/7 society. "The defining ethic in the modern workplace is more, bigger, faster. More information than ever is available to us and the speed of every transaction has increased exponentially, prompting a sense of permanent urgency and endless distraction" (Schwartz, et al., 2010, p. 3). With a focus on efficacy and efficiency, most organizations have neglected to realize that top managers are never satisfied. The "never enough" mentality has resulted in organizations investing more in their technology. Reich (2002) explains, "Computers, the internet, and digital commerce have exploded the old job categories into a vast array of new niches, creating a kaleidoscope of ways to make a living" (p. 71). These technologies "make instant communication possible anywhere, at any time, speed up decision making, create efficiencies, and fuel a truly global marketplace" (Schwartz, et al., 2010, p. 3). This dependency on technology can be detrimental to an organization's culture, morale, and mission. If the human resources of an organization are trained, educated, and motivated, they can potentially be more effective than a technological advancement that can easily become obsolete.

Human Resource Management

A firm's human resources are the people in an organization that are crucial to its performance and the quality of work life within it (Rainey, 2003, p. 219). "Unlike computers, human beings have the potential to grow and develop, to increase our depth, complexity and capacity over time" (Schwartz, et al., 2010, p. 5). Thus, managers and leaders should focus on investing and developing their human resources who have the capacity to make significant contributions to the organization's overall mission. Many organizations have noticed the importance of continuously training their employees and offering educational incentive programs to help keep employees up-to-date in their fields because "in a significant number of cases, people actually get worse at their jobs over time" (Schwartz, et al., 2010, p. 8). Performance can be enhanced if an employee is able to learn new ways of conceptualizing complex situations and deciphering abstract information. An employee should have knowledge of new research and advancements in his or her respective field in order to be able to adapt and overcome any organizational change. By performing at higher levels and being productive, an employee starts creating value for an organization. Most employees are evaluated by the value they create. Top managers seek employees who can bring value to an organization. When employees feel appreciated, they tend to perform at higher levels, producing more value (Kaifi, 2010). Unfortunately, most organizations are unable to "indulge" their employees and as a result, employees all over the world feel neglected and inundated. Interestingly enough, Schwartz, Jones, and McCarthy (2010) explain that:

> Only 38 percent of employees worldwide believe their senior managers are genuinely interested in their well-being. More than 50 percent feel they're treated as if they don't matter at all or that they're just another part of the organization to be managed. Only one out of every ten employees feels they're treated as vital corporate assets (p. 162).

With employees all over the world feeling like they "don't matter" in their organizations, it is important for upper level administrators continuously develop their leadership strategies. Furthermore, with organizations constantly evolving, strategic human resource management is the optimum way to enhance performance levels. "At IBM, for example, a thousand software developers working in different time zones have been given the flexibility to decide when they work" (Schwartz, et al., 2010, p. 230). Different strategies should be implemented in organizations all over the world to help "humanize" the workplace. Bolman and Deal (2003) explain that "many successful organizations have embraced creative and powerful ways to align individual and organizational needs. All these reflect the human resource frame's core assumptions by viewing the workforce as an investment rather than a cost" (p. 129). By the same token, employees must be committed to their organization. Developing organizational citizenship behavior attributes becomes significant for job security and stability. "Job satisfaction has been shown to be related to many other important personal and organizational outcomes. It is related to organizational citizenship behavior— behavior that is above and beyond the call of duty" (Nelson & Quick, 2011, p. 123). It must be mentioned that an employee should not expect a reward for their organizational citizenship behavior. Instead, an employee should understand that their actions will help the organization progress. For example, exceptional organizational citizens understand the importance of uniting, motivating, empowering, and helping their peers. Just like people are expected to be good citizens of society, they are also expected to be good citizens of organizations. Unfortunately, many workers routinely violate the policies and procedures of their organizations. Counterproductive behavior has become the norm in many organizations and as a result, organizations are implementing more stringent policies, enforcing regular trainings, and installing cameras throughout the workforce. Examples of counterproductive activities include daydreaming, looking busy, moonlighting, and even cyberloafing. When an employee is daydreaming, he or she appears to be working but is really distracted by non-work related thoughts and fantasies. When an employee is looking busy, he or she pretends to be busy or overwhelmed with work. An employee who is moonlighting uses company time and resources to complete personal tasks. An employee who is cyberloafing uses a company computer to send personal emails, chat online, or use the internet for their personal satisfaction. Consequently, "Some estimates suggest that typical cubicle dwellers stop what they are doing about once every three minutes to send e-mail, check Facebook or Twitter, surf over to YouTube, and so forth" (Colquitt, Lepine, & Wesson, 2011, p. 81). Cyberloafing tends to peak every March during the NCAA tournament, with estimates suggesting that employers lose $1.2 billion in lost productivity as employees watch or follow games online" (Colquitt, Lepine, & Wesson, 2011, p. 81). The following table represents signs of employee disengagement:

Signs of Being Physically Disengaged to an Organization
Table 1

Signs	Meaning to Management	Implications
Tardiness	Intentionally arriving to work late or leaving work early.	**Punctuality issues.**
Long or Excessive Breaks	Intentionally taking long breaks or too many breaks.	**Productivity issues.**
Missing Meetings	Intentionally neglecting important work functions.	**Reliability issues.**
Disregarding Deadlines	Intentionally being careless.	**Commitment issues.**
Excessive Absences	Intentionally disrupting the workflow.	**Dependability issues.**

High-quality organizational citizens refrain from counterproductive activities and being disengaged from their organization.

Non-Traditional Performance Strategies

In the 21st century, some managers and leaders believe that non-traditional strategies have the potential to enhance engagement, increase productivity, and improve performance levels in many organizations. For example, it is important to consider the importance of employees receiving the right amount of sleep each night which has a direct result on job performance. "At the most basic level, prolonged sleep deprivation has a negative impact on our health" and that sleep deprivation is the "equivalent to being legally intoxicated" (Schwartz, et al., 2010, pp. 60-61). Many researchers emphasize the importance of employees being well-rested as well as the importance of taking afternoon naps. What if managers allowed employees to take a nap after their lunch breaks? "Sleep is an important contributor to creative problem solving" (Nelson & Quick, 2011, p. 339). Could this strategy potentially help boost creativity and performance levels? Interestingly enough, "Perhaps no single daytime renewal behavior more reliably influences performance-and is less common in the workplace-than taking a nap" (Schwartz, et al., 2010, p. 72). Many researchers understand the correlation between being well-rested and higher performance levels and also point out the significance of taking time-off from work to relax. It is important to mention that Americans are sleeping less and are also taking less time off from work. "On average, Americans now fail to use 439 million paid vacations days a year. In 2008, one third of Americans said they intended to take no vacation at all" (Schwartz, et al., 2010, p. 75). In contrast,

Europeans continue to enjoy far more vacation time than Americans which relates to having a higher quality of work and home life. From an organizational behavior perspective, employees are usually overwhelmed with work and feel that they cannot take any quality time off to relax. The dilemma is that most employees will never feel as if they are all caught up and can truly enjoy a vacation.

The long-term implications of always being overwhelmed at work and never taking time off can result in disengagement and counterproductive activities. Organizations need healthy employees who are able to innovate, synergize, and work collectively with their peers. It is important to also mention that diet influences performance levels. Many organizations are notorious for spending thousands of dollars each month on purchasing unhealthy snacks for employees to encourage them to come to meetings or work extra hours. "The fast pace of today's work world has caused changes in people's eating patterns as well. Instead of eating meals jointly with family members, friends, and colleagues many families and individuals have been conditioned to eat in between work or other activities" (Mujtaba & McCartney, 2007, p. 1). As a result, many American employees are overweight, lethargic, and have lower performance levels. "Between 1960 and 2000, the average weight of American men between the ages of twenty-one and twenty-nine jumped from 163 to 191 pounds. During the same period, the average women went from 140 to 164" (Schwartz, et al., 2010, p. 91). It is important to emphasize that most organizations have several vending machines full of unhealthy snacks available for their employees. "The staple foods in most vending machines and at most off-sites are candy, cookies, and chips, filled with sugar, salt, and fat. These foods provide a quick and short-lived buzz when people's energy is flagging, but they take a toll on their health and productivity over time" (Schwartz, et al., 2010, p. 117). Organizations need to pay close attention to the food they offer in their vending machines and cafeterias. "Managing stress means managing one's food intake and having a regular exercise program" (Mujtaba & McCartney, 2007, p. 80). Some organizations have devoted significant resources to food and snacks that are offered at work. This non-traditional type of strategic human resource management is commendable and has many benefits for recruiting and retention.

The Johari Window

Managers understand that employees "connect" or "act" one way with their peers, a different way with their managers, a different way with their subordinates, and a completely different way with their family and friends. Joseph Luft and Harry Ingham (1955) developed a framework that is known as the Johari Window (named after its creators) which has four panes that demonstrate how one relates to others: open, blind, hidden, and unknown. The open pane contains information that a person knows about himself or herself and that he or she has no reason to hide, such as a person's physical features (e.g., eye color or height). The hidden pane contains personal information and feelings that a person is hiding from other people, such as a regretted tattoo or even a dream or career objective (e.g., becoming the CEO of the organization). The blind pane contains everything other people can see about a person, but the person can't see about himself or herself. For example, an individual may believe that he or she is a suboptimal leader but others may think that the individual is an outstanding leader. Finally, the unknown pane contains unknown talents, abilities, and attitudes a person may have. For example an individual who may have talents that have not been explored, such as being able to sing or play a difficult sport. Thus, through self-disclosure, an individual is able to open and close panes so that he or she can connect with others in a more meaningful manner. Table 2 illustrates the Johari Window:

Johari Window
Table 2

	Known to Self	**Not Known to Self**
Information Known to Others	*Open*	*Blind*
Information Not Known to Others	*Hidden*	*Unknown*

Psychologist Frederick Perls (1988) explained that "the purpose of self-disclosure is to own one's feelings, claiming one's own secrets in a way that allows people to be aware of them and content in them" (p. 1120). Those who fail to self-disclose, end up putting more pressure on themselves by having to constantly cover their tracks (e.g., lies), create false images, and end up preventing personal growth.

Two Outcomes of OB

As mentioned above, the two primary outcomes of organizational behavior are job performance (JP) and organizational commitment (OC). In order for an organization to be successful, there needs to be a "healthy" quality of work-life within the organization where employees feel valued, respected, and appreciated. Unfortunately, many organizations are known to be "toxic" by promoting an environment that is full of politics (e.g., nepotism or coercion), unjust practices (e.g., lack of transparency and accountability), and workforce bullying (e.g., scare tactics and manipulation). In the past, many managers believed that emphasizing the importance of job performance and organizational commitment would automatically result in a healthier quality of work-life. In reality, contemporary managers understand that the quality of work-life has the ability to either positively or negatively influence job performance and organizational commitment. As an example, Cisco System employees "point to the fun workplace culture as a key factor, with company cafes offering movie-themed menus at Academy Awards time or "nerd lunches" during which experts discuss important tech topics" (Colquitt, Lepine, & Wesson, 2011, p. 74). As a result, Cisco Systems enjoys one of the lowest voluntary turnover rates in its industry—around 3 percent. In management philosophy, there needs to be a paradigm shift to where a manager's most important task is creating a healthier quality of work-life through successful leadership. Chapter 3 will discuss a number of different leadership styles that can be used for creating a healthy organization.

Philosophers and scholars have theorized for centuries about the correlation between job performance and organizational commitment. Figure 4 illustrates the two outcomes of organizational behavior.

Two Outcomes of OB
Figure 4

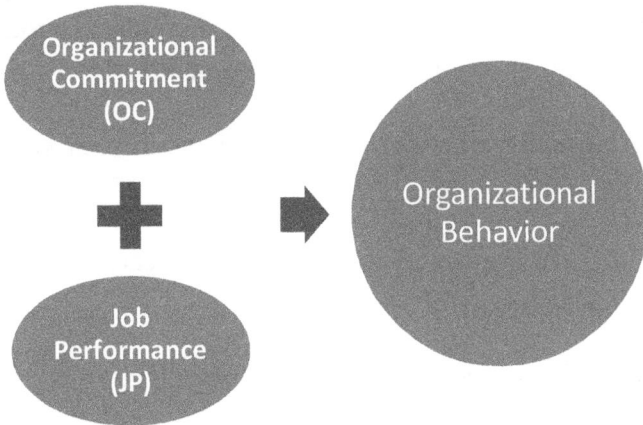

Job Performance (Chapter 4) can be simply described as the value of the set of employee behaviors that contribute to task accomplishment. Organizational Commitment (Chapter 5) can be easily described as the desire on the part of an employee to remain a devoted member of an organization.

Summary

Chapter 2 discussed the importance of human resources in organizations. In addition, non-traditional performance strategies were addressed for managers and leaders to take into consideration. A number of examples were used to help illustrate key points.

Chapter Review Questions

1. Why are human resources so important to organizations?

2. Do you agree with the Johari Window? Justify your response.

3. What are some examples of counterproductive activities that you have witnessed?

4. What non-traditional performance strategies would you implement as a leader of an organization?

5. What kind of snacks would you have in your vending machines at work?

6. Why is it important for employees to eat healthy and exercise regularly?

7. Why do you act different when interacting with your manager, friends, and family?

8. Do you agree with the statement: Only 38 percent of employees worldwide believe their senior managers are genuinely interested in their well-being? Please justify your response.

9. Do you "live to work" or "work to live"? Explain why.

10. Would you agree that quality of work-life can enhance job performance and organizational commitment? Please justify your response.

Discussion Questions

1. What will an organization be like 50 years from now?

2. Should cyberloafing and moonlighting be allowed in organizations?

3. Discuss why a dependency on technology can be detrimental to organizational behavior.

Case Study

Mary Johnson was recently hired for a management position at *Company XYZ*. Based on her past experiences, Mary believes that all employees are productive, responsible, and look forward to new challenges. On her first day, she notices many strange behaviors taking place in her new department. For example, her secretary is on Facebook throughout the day, the assistant manager jammed the copy machine because he was printing out his 250-page doctoral dissertation, and an employee took a two-hour long lunch break. She isn't sure whether or not to reprimand these employees because she remembers the importance of creating a quality work life.

Later in the day, she receives an email from the VP of the company who brings to her attention that her new department has a reputation of submitting all reports late. She is troubled and calls her friend who is an "organizational development doctor" to help analyze and diagnose her department's ailments.

Case Questions

1. What questions would the organizational development doctor ask Mary Johnson?

2. What questions would the organizational development doctor ask employees?

3. Based on the case, who do you think is at fault? Explain why.

4. Conduct a RED Analysis on this case and explain your findings.

5. How can the work of Robert Owen, Andrew Ure, and Elton Mayo be applied to this case?

Special Case Assignment

Suppose that Mary Johnson went home that evening and created a short survey to hand out to each employee the following morning. Her goal is to make things "better" in her department.

Create a 10 question survey relating to productivity, with a 5-point scale (ranging from strongly disagree to strongly agree) for each question, that could be used to yield important data for Mary Johnson.

3

ORGANIZATIONAL LEADERSHIP

Today's competitive organizations demand leadership. Leadership is about behavior first and skills second. It all comes back to promoting positive expectations and having these expectations realized. Leaders believe in change and energize organizations to innovate continuously. They recognize the need for synergy, and emphasize the importance of unity and collaboration. Schwartz, Jones, & McCarthy (2010) explain, "Many organizations build leadership programs around competency models, a list of core skills they expect all leaders to cultivate" (p. 29). Organizations need employees who can be molded into leaders that will be able to influence others to complete tasks and follow the mission of the organization. Rath and Conchie (2009) discuss the three variables to becoming an effective leader: knowing your strengths and investing in others', getting the people with the right strengths on your team, and understanding and meeting the four basic needs of those who seek leadership. Rath and Conchie (2009) state, "Organizations are quick to look for leaders who are great communicators, visionary thinkers, and who can also get things done and follow through" (p. 7). There are many different types of leaders: servant leaders, transactional leaders, transformational leaders, situational leaders, democratic leaders, laissez-faire leaders, autocratic leaders, and many other variations.

According to Rath and Conchie (2009), there is a "correlation between awareness of one's strengths and the subsequent increase in self-confidence" (p. 16). If a leader is self-confident, he or she will gain the respect of his or her peers by being able to make sound decisions that will be in the best interest of the organization. Self-confidence has proven to be a strength that can help a person in various ways. Kaifi (2010) explains, "Learn to accept yourself. Self-acceptance means learning to believe in your heart that you are valuable and that your differences from others are more of a plus than a minus" (p.160). Furthermore, "By embracing our own opposites and getting comfortable with our contradictions, we build richer, deeper lives. This is especially crucial for leaders, who must weigh multiple points of view, balance conflicting priorities, serve numerous constituencies, and make decisions about issues with no easy answers" (Schwartz, et al., 2010, p. 29). Consequently, "people who are aware of their strengths and build self-confidence at a young age may reap a cumulative advantage that continues to grow over a lifetime" (Rath & Conchie, 2009, p. 16). This initial experience, will prepare individuals for when they enter the workforce.

Organizations understand that leaders must be able to communicate in order to be effective. In fact, President Gerald Ford once remarked, "If I went back to college again, I'd concentrate on two areas: learning to write and to speak before an audience. Nothing in life is more important than the ability to communicate effectively" (Maxwell, 2010, p. 7). Leaders can learn to develop certain skills which can help them become more effective, efficient, and productive. It is important for a leader to know his or her own strengths just as a "carpenter knows his tools" (Rath & Conchie, 2009, p. 13). A leader must focus on enhancing each strength and developing each weakness in order to be able to create success. Rath and Conchie (2009) explain the value of "leaders knowing their own strengths and also reveal how important it is for leaders to help others uncover their own strengths as early as possible" (p. 16). It is important to mention that the sooner one learns about his or her leadership strengths, the more successful he or she will be in all aspects of life. It's all about "making key behaviors automatic" (Schwartz, et al., 2010, p. 37).

Rath and Conchie (2009) explain how the most effective leaders rally a broader group of people toward an organization's goals, mission, and objectives. Over the years, many researchers have posed an important question: Why do people follow? According to legendary investor Warren Buffet, "A leader is someone who can get things done through other people." Rath and Conchie (2009) explain the four basic needs of followers: trust, compassion, stability, and hope. The authors added, "The followers we surveyed also cited honesty, integrity, and respect as distinct contributions from the leaders in their lives" (Rath & Conchie, 2009, p. 83). The trust factor is important when working in groups because it takes time to establish trust among a group of people. Once trust is established, a group will become more productive because each person can count or depend on the other. Respect, integrity, and honesty are the outcomes of strong relationships built on trust. Rath and Conchie (2009) stress the importance of leaders caring about each of their employees by showing genuine compassion for the people they lead. Rath and Conchie (2009) explain, "Caring, friendship, happiness, and love were other frequently mentioned words followers used when asked what leaders contribute to their lives" (p. 85). It is important to understand that "as you take the role of a caring leader, people soon begin relating to you differently" (Kouzes & Posner, 2003, p. 77). Strong leaders care about the well-being of each employee while inside and outside of the organization. Interestingly enough, successful leaders encourage subordinates "to put their family first" (Rath & Conchie, 2009, p. 86). This humanistic approach contributes to a healthier quality of work life (QWL). "Being able to deliver a warm style of leadership and paying attention to others are key elements of gaining the trust and respect of one's peers" (Kaifi, 2010, p. 11). Consequently, William Ouchi (1981) developed Theory Z which is a hybrid style of management that combines characteristics of Japanese and American management styles by focusing on trust and intimacy in the workplace and treating employees like family.

The best leaders are the ones that can be counted on in times of need. Ultimately, it is important for a leader to offer stability and confidence. Employees expect to know where their career is headed and how the organization is doing financially. Rath and Conchie (2009) explain, "Employees who have high confidence in their company's financial future are nine times as likely to be engaged in their jobs when compared to those who have lower confidence about their organization's financial future" (Rath & Conchie, 2009, p. 87). Instilling hope may seem like an obvious requirement for leading others. Hope gives followers something to look forward to, and it helps them see a way through chaos and complexity. "Knowing that things can and will be better in the future is a powerful motivator" (Rath & Conchie, 2009, p. 89). When hope is absent, people lose confidence, disengage, and often feel helpless.

Many researchers believe that there are four domains of leadership strengths: executing, influencing, relationship building, and strategic thinking. For example, Wendy Kopp of *Teach for America* is known for her executing skills and creating an organization from scratch; while Simon Cooper of *The Ritz Carlton* is recognized for his influencing skills and transforming the organization to a new level of excellence. Mervyn Davies of *Standard Chartered Bank* is known for his relationship building capabilities and his beliefs in investing even more time and money in developing his people. And, Brad Anderson of *Best Buy* is recognized for his strategic thinking skills that helped to take a previously unknown regional electronics store and turn it into the largest consumer electronics retailer in America. Many professionals agree that it is important for leaders to be able to analyze their "use of time" throughout the day (Kaifi, 2011, p. 63). One common denominator amongst many leaders is the utilization of "daily to-do lists" that help with organizing and prioritizing tasks to ensure the highest level of productivity. In addition, leadership programs have become the norm for many organizations who value effective leaders.

Lifecycle of Leadership Development

There are four "E" stages to the "Lifecycle of Leadership Development" process that potential leaders experience. The most basic stage is the *embryonic leader*. This is when leaders observe the leadership skills of others. The next stage is the *evolving leader*. This is when leaders develop or "fine-tune" their natural propensity to influence, motivate, and empower followers. The third stage is the *effective leader*. This is when leaders feel comfortable leading teams, making big decisions, and creating new opportunities. And the final stage is the *enlightening leader*. This is when seasoned leaders are able to influence or teach new leaders who are at the embryonic stage. This ongoing cycle produces leaders who are able to reach the enlightening stage and give back to others. Figure 5 depicts the Lifecycle of Leadership Development:

Lifecycle of Leadership Development
Figure 5

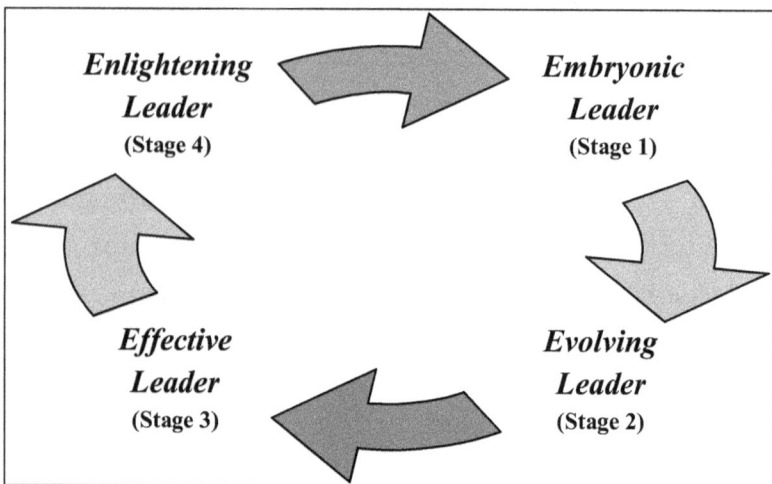

In some organizations, leaders start at the embryonic stage and then gradually move on to the evolving stage and are unable to eventually make the transition to the effective and enlightening stages. If there is a shortage of leaders at the enlightening stage, the organization will face many organizational obstacles resulting in organizational politics. Some examples of organizational politics are: having allies, lack of opportunity and training, too much bureaucracy, the glass ceiling phenomenon, and nepotism. These are only some of the reasons for the hindrance in leadership development in certain organizations. Organizational politics is the "use of power and influence in organizations" (Nelson & Quick, 2011, p. 377). It must be mentioned that the term "organizational politics" has a negative connotation but can be positive depending on the situation.

Three Classic Leadership Styles

The earliest research on leadership styles was conducted by Kurt Lewin (1939) and his students who identified three basic styles: autocratic, democratic, and laissez-faire. The *autocratic style* is directive, assertive, aggressive, and controlling in relationships. Leaders with an autocratic style use strict policies and procedures to control the work environment. Followers have little power and are unable to challenge authority. The leader with a *democratic style* is open-minded, interactive, egalitarian, and collaborative, and focuses on policies and procedures less than the autocratic leader. Followers are a part of the decision-making process at all levels. The leader with a *laissez-faire style* uses a hands-off approach, giving followers a significant amount of autonomy to complete tasks, determine goals, and make decisions. This type of leader focuses on policies and procedures less than the democratic leader. It should be mentioned that the laissez-faire style can be "risky" and can create chaos for followers due to a lack of supervision.

Classic Leadership Styles
Figure 6

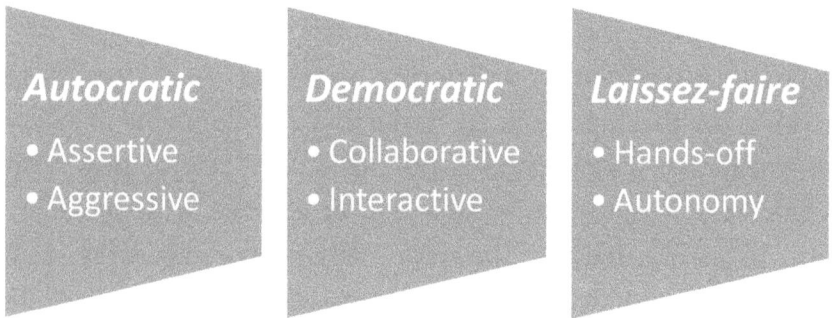

Autocratic	Democratic	Laissez-faire
• Assertive	• Collaborative	• Hands-off
• Aggressive	• Interactive	• Autonomy

A general in the military may have an autocratic style of leading, while the dean of a college may have a democratic style of leading, and a retail manager may have a laissez-faire style of leading. Over the years, there have been many debates over leadership styles and whether or not leaders should be focused on completing "tasks" or building healthy "relationships" in the workplace.

Leadership Style Approach

There are two important behaviors related to leadership style: task and relationship. *Task behaviors* facilitate goal accomplishment by helping group members achieve their objectives (Northouse, 2004, p. 65). It is important for a leader to think about the "tasks of the organization by figuring out the most efficient, effective, and productive way to complete all tasks" (Kaifi, 2009, p. 92). Moreover, Vroom (1973) explains, "All managers are decision makers. Furthermore, their effectiveness as managers is largely reflected in their track record in making right decisions. These right decisions in turn largely depend on whether or not the manager has utilized the right person or persons in the right ways in helping him solve the problem" (p. 66). *Relationship behaviors* help "subordinates feel comfortable with themselves, with each other, and with the situation in which they find themselves" (Northouse, 2004, p. 65). Finding the optimum way to lead has been the principal goal of many researchers at several universities. Over the years, a number of surveys have been created for measuring task and relationship orientations. For example, Northouse (2004) shares a convenient survey instrument (please see below) that has been used by a number of researchers (e.g., Mujtaba 2008; Tajaddini & Mujtaba, 2009; Mujtaba & Kaifi, 2010; Mujtaba, Khanfar, & Khanfar, 2010). Depending on the demographic questions that are asked, researchers are able to correlate task and relationship orientations to gender, religion, ethnicity, management experience, and many other variables.

Leadership Style Questionnaire Instructions

To determine your dominant personal leadership style, circle one of the following options that best describes how you see yourself (or the person that is being evaluated) regarding each statement. For each statement, you can indicate the degree to which you (or the person being evaluated) engage(s) in the stated behavior. A rating of 1 means "Never" and a rating of 5 means "Always" regarding a person demonstrating the specific behavior. The questionnaire is on the following page.

Leadership Style Questionnaire
Figure 7

"A" Style and Orientation

Questions	Never...................Always
1. Tells group members what they are supposed to do.	1 2 3 4 5
2. Sets standards of performance for group members.	1 2 3 4 5
3. Makes suggestions about how to solve problems.	1 2 3 4 5
4. Makes his or her perspective clear to others.	1 2 3 4 5
5. Develops a plan of action for the group.	1 2 3 4 5
6. Defines role responsibilities for each group member.	1 2 3 4 5
7. Clarifies his or her own role within the group.	1 2 3 4 5
8. Provides a plan for how the work is to be done.	1 2 3 4 5
9. Provides criteria for what is expected of the group.	1 2 3 4 5
10. Encourages group members to do high-quality work.	1 2 3 4 5
Total Score for "A" Orientation:	

"B" Style and Orientation

Questions	Never...................Always
1. Acts friendly with members of the group.	1 2 3 4 5
2. Helps others feel comfortable in the group.	1 2 3 4 5
3. Responds favorably to suggestions made by others.	1 2 3 4 5
4. Treats others fairly.	1 2 3 4 5
5. Behaves in a predictable manner toward group.	1 2 3 4 5
6. Communicates actively with group members.	1 2 3 4 5
7. Shows concern for the well-being of others.	1 2 3 4 5
8. Shows flexibility in making decisions.	1 2 3 4 5
9. Discloses thoughts and feelings to group members.	1 2 3 4 5
10. Helps group members get along.	1 2 3 4 5
Total Score for "B" Orientation:	

A = Task Orientation Scores: _____   **B = Relationship** Orientation Scores: _____

- 45-50   Very high range
- 40-44   High range
- 35-39   Moderately high range
- 30-34   Moderately low range
- 25-29   Low range
- 10-24   Very low range

The Ohio State Leadership Studies

In the late 1940s, the leadership research program at Ohio State measured specific leadership behaviors. The researchers had subordinates complete questionnaires about their leaders by using the Leader Behavior Description Questionnaire (LBDQ). Researchers found that subordinates' responses on the questionnaire clustered around two underlying dimensions of leader behaviors: *initiating structure* and *consideration* (Stogdill, 1974). Initiating structure behaviors were essentially "task" behaviors focused on getting work completed as efficiently as possible. On the other hand, consideration behaviors were essentially "relationship" behaviors focused on building friendships. Around the same time, researchers at the University of Michigan were also investigating leadership behavior.

University of Michigan Leadership Studies

The Michigan studies revealed two types of leadership behaviors: *employee orientation* and *production orientation.* Surprisingly, those studies revealed similar concepts to initiating structure and consideration. Employee orientation describes the behaviors of leaders who approach followers or subordinates with a humanistic perspective or "relationship" orientation. On the other hand, production orientation describes the behaviors of leaders who focus on productivity and efficiency or "task" orientation. Northouse (2004) explains, "Unlike the Ohio State researchers, the Michigan researchers, in their initial studies, conceptualized employee and production orientations as opposite ends of a single continuum" and further explains, "that leaders who were oriented toward production were less oriented to employees, and those who were employee oriented were less production oriented" (p. 68). Since then, researchers have used this framework to better understand the behaviors of leaders from different cultures (Mujtaba & Kaifi, 2010; Tajaddini & Mujtaba, 2009). There are several key traits that contribute to a leader's success.

Ethos, Logos, and Pathos

Many centuries ago, Greek philosopher Aristotle wrote about the importance of *ethos*, *logos*, and *pathos*. These broad and simple constructs can be used when addressing most leadership traits. Projecting a positive ethos (character) is significant for leaders when influencing followers because followers seek leaders with whom they can connect. For example, a leader with a positive ethos may be ethical, trustworthy, or credible. Utilizing logos (logic) is important for a leader who is in charge of making conceptual decisions. Leaders who possess high levels of logos are respected and valued by their followers. It should be mentioned that depending too much on logos and not enough on ethos can be detrimental. Maxwell (2010) provides a case in point: "Consider the differences in connecting skill between Ronald Reagan and Jimmy Carter when they ran against one another. In their final debate on October 28, 1980, Carter came across as cold and impersonal. To every question he was asked, Carter responded with facts and figures" (p. 5). Those who watched this revolutionary debate realized that they could connect with Ronald Reagan, and as a result, were more inclined to vote for him. Leaders who are able to control their own pathos (emotions) and the pathos of followers have been known to be effective leaders. This concept relates to emotional intelligence. Figure 8 illustrates the lifecycle of leadership development based upon different levels of ethos, logos, and pathos.

Lifecycle of Leadership Development: Ranks and Traits
Figure 8

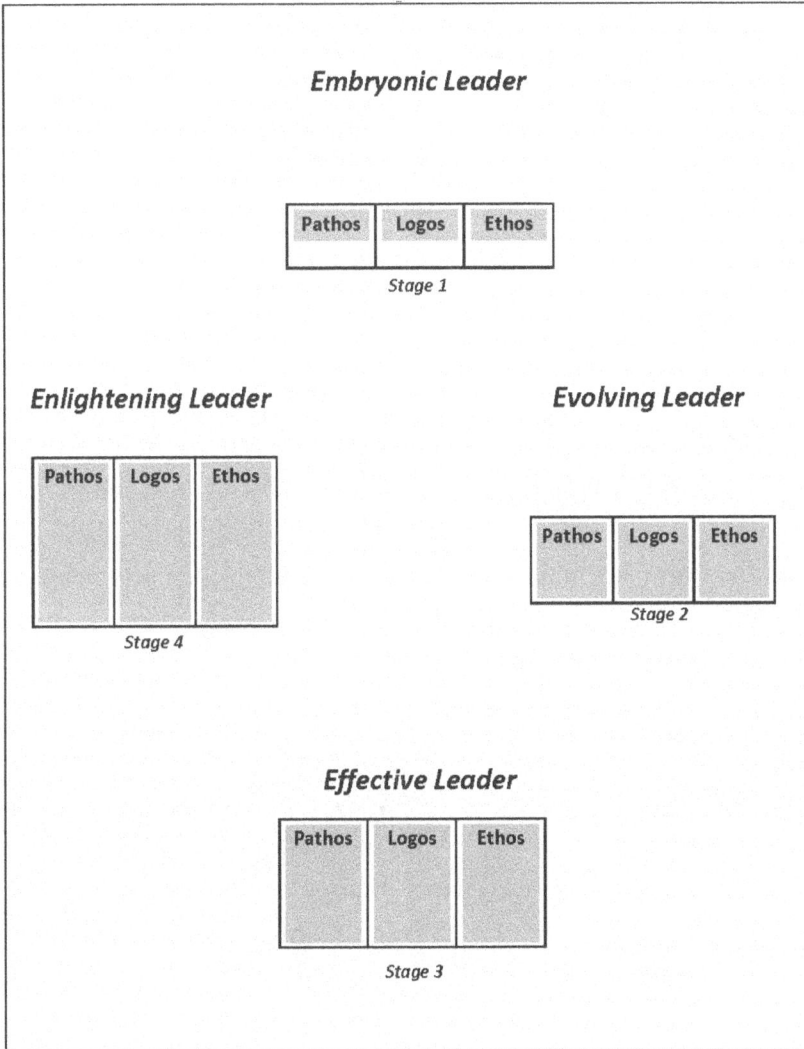

As can be seen in Figure 8, the embryonic leader in the first stage has low levels of pathos, logos, and ethos. At the second stage, the evolving leader starts to develop his or her pathos, logos, and ethos levels. At the third stage, the effective leader has moderately high levels of pathos, logos, and ethos in order to be an "effective" leader. In the final stage, the enlightening leader has significantly high levels of pathos, logos, and ethos and is ready to "enlighten" new leaders. Most important of all, an enlightening leader must master the art of communicating clearly in order to effectively influence followers. "According to Lawrence Kohlberg's moral development theory, people become morally mature as they age and socialize in an ethical environment" (Mujtaba & Kaifi, 2010, p. 35).

Leadership and Communication

There is a high demand for leaders who are able to communicate effectively. An early Harvard Business School study on what it takes to achieve success and be promoted in an organization emphasized the importance of communicating, making sound decisions, and getting things done with and through people (Bowman et al., 1964). According to Maxwell (2010), "People cannot succeed in life without communicating effectively" (p. 2).Unfortunately, many leaders have overlooked this important concept and are unable to connect to others while communicating. In today's global society, it is important for leaders to be able to connect with their followers because it creates an atmosphere of unity, equality, and transparency. A leader should realize that he or she has successfully connected with followers when he or she senses: extra effort (followers go the extra mile), unsolicited appreciation (positive things are said), increased communication (followers express themselves more readily), enjoyable experiences (followers feel good about what they're doing), emotional bondedness (a connection on an emotional level is displayed), positive energy (followers' "emotional" batteries are charged by being together), growing synergy (followers' effectiveness is greater than the sum of contributions), and finally, unconditional love (followers are accepting leadership without reservation). In order for organizations to continuously improve and innovate, leaders should master the art of connecting to others because of both the short-term and long-term implications it will have on job performance, organizational commitment, and quality of work-life.

By connecting to others in the workforce, employees feel empowered and valued, resulting in higher productivity and performance levels. Maxwell (2010) explains, "Connecting is the ability to identify with people and relate to them in a way that increases your influence on them" (p. 3). This strategy of connecting, appreciating, and valuing others in the workforce can be a more useful intrinsic reward or incentive for enhancing productivity levels when compared to extrinsic cash incentives (which has become the norm in many organizations). Thus, by recognizing employees and humanizing the workforce, leaders are actually reinforcing the fact that connecting to others equates to everyone being respected and valued.

Leaders who are able to communicate well and connect to others are able to influence followers on a deeper and personal level. "Leadership communication is the controlled, purposeful transfer of meaning by which leaders influence a single person, a group, an organization, or a community" (Barrett, 2008, p. 5). Furthermore, Maxwell (2010) states, "All great communication has one thing in common: the speaker said something that people remembered long after the talk was finished" (p. 184). In addition, Maxwell (2010) prescribes the following advice, "If you already work at connecting with people, you can learn to become even better at it. And if you haven't previously tried to connect with others, you will be astounded by how it can change your life" (p. 17). Connecting to others should become an automatic skill for all people and leaders alike.

When connecting to followers, it is important to understand that a leader can connect to followers in different settings. A leader can connect with followers at three different levels: one-on-one, in a group, and with an audience. When connecting one-on-one, it is important to talk more about the other person and less about yourself. When connecting in a group, look for ways to compliment people in the group for their ideas and actions. And finally, when connecting with an audience, let your listeners know that you are excited to be with them (Maxwell, 2010, pp. 20-21). Each level of connecting requires different levels of energy. Maxwell (2010) states, "Connecting always requires energy. The larger the group, the more energy that's required to connect" (p. 93). Some researchers explain that "the effectiveness of communication plays an important role in determining whether there is process gain or process loss" (Colquitt, Lepine, & Wesson, 2010, p. 422). Maxwell (2010) explains that connecting and communicating effectively on an intellectual level requires knowing two things: "your subject and yourself" (p. 62). People have a short attention span, which is why it is so important to use the connecting strategy. If the audience can relate to what is being said, they are more likely to listen. Maxwell (2010) explains, "People can perceive a lot in seven seconds. They can decide that they do not want to hear anything a speaker has to say, or they can be struck by how much they are attracted to someone" (p. 55).

Effective communicators are also well groomed and dressed which relates to a leader's outer image. "If you're well groomed and wearing the right clothing for your situation, then that's a good start" (Maxwell, 2010, p. 55). Similarly, it is important for a great communicator to be able to use facial expressions to convey specific messages. Maxwell (2010) explains how, "Great actors can tell an entire story without uttering a word, simply by using facial expressions (p. 56). Moreover, effective communicators are able to share experiences to which others can relate. For example, a leader trying to connect to his or her followers can explain how he or she has been in their shoes and more importantly, can relate to their experiences. "Leadership communication uses the full range of communication skills and resources to overcome interferences and to create and deliver messages that guide, direct, motivate, or inspire other to action" (Barrett, 2008, p. 5). This simple connecting factor of relating to the experiences of others can help a leader promote higher standards, enhance morale, and advance performance levels within an organization. Maxwell (2010) states, "There's no substitute for personal experience when we want to connect with people's hearts" (p. 63). Moreover, "Human beings just don't put their hearts into something they don't believe in" (Kouzes & Posner, 2003, p. 49). Connecting to people's hearts is the most powerful medium for connecting. Leaders who have an ethical image and who are trusted by their followers are able to influence more people. Maxwell (2010) offers, "Trust plays the same role in all relationships, and it always impacts communication. To be an effective connector over the long haul, you have to establish credibility by living what you communicate" and further states, "If you don't, you undermine trust, people disconnect from you, and they stop listening (p. 231). "Effective communicators are comfortable in their own skin.

They're confident because they know what they can and can't do, and they gravitate to their communication sweet spot when they speak to people" (Maxwell, 2010, p. 63).

A prime example of an effective leader and communicator who was able to connect with millions of people was Martin Luther King Jr. In his book, Maxwell (2010) states, "Listen to Martin Luther King Jr. and you will be inspired by his words. Words are the currency of ideas and have the power to change the world" (p. 67). Great leaders are able to connect to others by continuously emphasizing key points. Maxwell (2010) offers the following advice,

> If you are communicating with others, whether you're speaking to a child, leading a meeting, or giving a speech to a large audience, your goal should be to get to the point as soon as you have established a connection with people and to make as great an impact on others as you can with as few words as possible. Great leaders and speakers do this consistently (p. 160).

Leaders are also known to be unpredictable when they are communicating. "When leaders unequivocally communicate standards, they honor everyone's desire to do their very best. They elevate the human spirit" (Kouzes & Posner, 2003, p. 59). "The more predictable listeners think you are, the lower the impact you make on them. Conversely, if you lower your predictability, you increase your impact" (Maxwell, 2010, p. 185). When communicating, it is also imperative to emphasize the importance of timing, the use of right words, leaving a lasting impression, and making the experience enjoyable. Maxwell (2010) explains, "Timing is often the difference between success and failure in an endeavor. Good communicators understand the importance of the right words" (p. 222). Furthermore, "All great communication has one thing in common: the speaker said something that people remembered long after the talk was finished" (p. 184). In addition, "Perhaps the most effective way to capture people's interest and make the experience enjoyable when you talk is to include stories" (p. 191). Over the years, several types of leadership styles have emerged: servant, transactional, transformational, and situational, among many others. The leader-member exchange theory describes how "leader-member relationships develop over time on a dyadic basis" (Colquitt, Lepine, & Wesson, 2011, p. 463).

Servant Leadership

Servant leadership is a popular and unique leadership behavior that has proven to be effective for many leaders and followers. Robert Greenleaf (1970) first presented the term "servant leadership" in a 1970 essay, entitled "The Servant Leader" where he stated that servant leadership "begins with the natural feeling that one wants to serve, to serve first. Then conscious choice brings one to aspire to lead" (p. 7). Many servant leaders believe that the overall objective of the organization or community can be accomplished if followers are nurtured. "Servant leadership emphasizes that leaders should be attentive to the concerns of their followers and empathize with them; they should take care of them and nurture them" (Northouse, 2004, p. 309). A servant leader leads by pure example and provides "appropriate tools, equipment, and other resources so the followers can be successful in their completion of assigned tasks" (Winston & Patterson, 2006, p. 9). Servant leaders do not rely on their power or authority, and instead rely on their innate abilities to promote equality, trust, respect, and collaboration. Mother Teresa's humanitarian work in India is an example of servant leadership. She was awarded the Nobel Peace Prize in 1979.

Transactional Leadership

Transactional leadership is an "exchange" that occurs between a leader and a follower. For example, "politicians who win votes by promising no new taxes are demonstrating transactional leadership" (Northouse, 2004, p. 170). Interestingly enough, James MacGregor Burns (1978) was one of the first researchers to discuss both transactional and transformational leadership. From a pragmatic perspective, it can be conceptualized as a "business transaction" that occurs between two parties. Transactional leadership assumes that "followers agree about achieving the required goals and objectives in exchange for rewards or praise" (Farag et al., 2009, p. 27). Transactional leaders are successful because of their ability to entice and motivate followers. At times, followers need a reason to perform a task. "Transactional leadership refers to the bulk of leadership models, which focus on the exchanges that occur between leaders and their followers" (Northouse, 2004, p. 170). An example of a transactional leader is Barack Obama (44th President of the United States). During his 2008 campaign, Obama promised to "extend the Bush tax cuts for lower incomes" in exchange for support and votes.

Transformational Leadership

Transformational leadership is a dynamic leadership behavior that "inspires" followers and also "transforms" the way followers think. "Transformational leadership has been widely researched from many perspectives, including a series of qualitative studies of prominent leaders and CEOs in large, well-known organizations" and "has also been the focal point for a large body of leadership research since its introduction in the 1970s" (Northouse, 2004, p. 183). Transformational leaders are able to create a clear vision for followers. Pounder (2008) explains transformational leadership outcomes when reframing an organization by stating, "the effect of transformational leadership on subordinates centers on three leadership outcomes: (a) the ability of the leader to generate extra effort on the part of those being led, (b) subordinates' perception of leader effectiveness, and (c) their satisfaction with the leader" (p. 2). Transformational leaders are known for empowering followers. According to Farag, McGuinness, and Anthony (2009), "Transformational leaders achieve organizational goals by empowering staff who are committed to the same organizational goals" (p. 27). As with any type of leadership, "transformational leadership involves an exceptional form of influence that moves followers to accomplish more than what is usually expected of them. It is a process that often incorporates charismatic and visionary leadership" (Northouse, 2004, p. 169). An example of a transformational leader is Mohandas (Mahatma) Gandhi who was nominated for the Nobel Peace Prize five times. Gandhi was able to influence his followers in India to "peacefully" reclaim their land from the British. This "transformation" from violent to non-violent protests had many positive implications and outcomes. A different transformational leader was President John F. Kennedy. On May 25, 1961, President Kennedy announced before a special joint session of Congress the ambitious goal of sending an American safely to the moon before the end of the decade. In 1969, this near-impossible goal was accomplished. President Kennedy was able to influence and transform the US into a disciplined, motivated, and unified society.

Situational Leadership

Situational leadership was originally developed by Paul Hersey and Kenneth Blanchard (1969). As the name implies, situational leadership requires adapting to situations that arise because the "situational contingencies dictate your style for that moment" (Lumsden, Lumsden, & Wiethoff, 2010, p. 258). "Situational leadership stresses that leadership is composed of both a directive and supportive dimension, and each has to be applied appropriately in a given situation" (Northouse, 2004, p. 87). The directive dimension is similar to "task behaviors" and the supportive dimension is similar to "relationship behaviors" (as discussed above). "Situational leadership stresses that leaders need to find out about their subordinates' needs and then adapt their style accordingly" (Northouse, 2004, p. 93). For example, if subordinates are lacking confidence, then the situational approach suggests that the leader should lead with a supporting style for optimum outcomes. "Although many theories of leadership are descriptive in nature, the situational approach is prescriptive. It tells you what you should and should not do in various contexts" (Northouse, 2004, p. 93). The three core competencies of a situational leader are: diagnosing, flexibility, and partnering. "It seems, then, that flexibility in leadership style is a necessity if a high level of leadership effectiveness is desired and required by the situation" (Silverthorne & Wang, 2001, p. 400). An example of a situational leader is a football coach who is able to adapt to each game of the season by diagnosing the situation, being flexible to the differences in the games, and partnering with his or her team for a positive outcome.

Summary

Chapter 3 discussed the importance of effective organizational leadership. For example, different leadership styles can be used for enhancing productivity levels. This chapter also addressed the different traits that experienced leaders possess and the lifecycle of leadership development. A number of examples were used to help illustrate key points.

Chapter Review Questions

1. What strengths should leaders have and why?

2. What are some of your strengths that make you a great leader?

3. What are some issues with Theory Z?

4. Where are you in the "Lifecycle of Leadership Development" process?

5. Of the three classical leadership styles, which do you prefer as a follower and why? Which style would you use as a leader and why?

6. As a leader, would you focus on tasks or relationships? Why?

7. When influencing and persuading followers, would you depend more on your ethos, logos, or pathos? Please justify your response.

8. Why is it important for leaders to be effective communicators? How are your communication skills?

9. What are the differences between servant leadership and situational leadership?

10. What are the differences between transactional leadership and transformational leadership?

Discussion Questions

1. What type of a leadership style should the President of the US have?

2. Do you think leaders are born or leaders are made?

3. Discuss how a leader could influence followers without power. How exactly would that influence take place?

Case Study

Kevin Michaels is a manager and "servant leader" at *Company XYZ* and is known for being a caring and nurturing with his followers. He recognizes the value of Theory Z. The CEO of *Company XYZ* does not agree with Kevin's "spoiling and nurturing" mentality for a number of reasons. At the last management meeting, the CEO pulled Kevin aside and explained to him that he "is a push-over and that he needs to change his leadership style." To make matters worse, Kevin has a problem with procrastinating, delegating work, and motivating himself and others. Certain tasks that his department is responsible for are not being completed each day. After a day of reflecting, Kevin comes to the conclusion that it would be beneficial to change his leadership style but isn't sure where to start and what to do. He is stumped and calls his friend who is an "organizational development doctor" to analyze and diagnose the situation.

Case Questions

1. Do you agree that Kevin Michaels (a servant leader) should focus on his shortcomings first? Why or why not?

2. What questions would the organizational development doctor ask Kevin Michaels?

3. What questions would the organizational development doctor ask Kevin's employees?

4. Conduct a RED Analysis on this case and explain your findings.

5. How can the work of Aristotle, James MacGregor Burns, and Kurt Lewin be applied to this case?

Special Case Assignment

Suppose that Kevin Michaels went home that evening and created a short survey to hand out to each employee the following morning. His goal is to make things "better" in his department.

Create a 10 question survey instrument with a 5-point scale (ranging from strongly disagree to strongly agree) for each question relating to transformational leadership that could be used to yield important data for Kevin Michaels.

4

Job Performance

Job performance is formally defined as the set of employee behaviors that contribute to organizational goal accomplishment. Job performance is almost never one-dimensional. "What you measure is probably more critical to the control process than how you measure it" (Robbins & DeCenzo, 2007, p. 156). For example, a basketball player is assessed based upon his or her positive attributes in a number of different areas (e.g., points, assists, and rebounds per game). A basketball player is also assessed based upon his or her negative attributes in a number of different areas (e.g., personal fouls, technical fouls, and ejections). Also, an important criterion such as "sportsmanship" may be a positive or negative area for a basketball player. The different areas of a job that are usually assessed are also known as the job criteria. According to Mathis and Jackson (1994), "Each job criterion should be compared with a performance standard, which is the expected level of performance" (p. 327). The Job Performance Framework (Figure 14) has three main categories (citizen-based, task-based, and outcome-based) and several sub-categories. A citizen-based criterion identifies subjective character traits such as being personable, caring, helpful, and courteous. A task-based criterion identifies the ability of an employee to complete tasks in an efficient, productive, and effective manner. Finally, an outcome-based criterion identifies the quality of the tasks that have been completed. All three complement one another and have been proven to be key areas of analysis and assessment for many employers. According to Lamberton and Minor (2010), "Experts are now becoming aware that the connections among job satisfaction and employee turnover, absenteeism, overall performance are not so simple" (pp. 90-91). It must be mentioned that employees who dominate in one area (but not the others) are usually considered "sub-optimal" employees. Figure 9 illustrates the three broad criteria relevant to job performance.

Job Performance Criteria
Figure 9

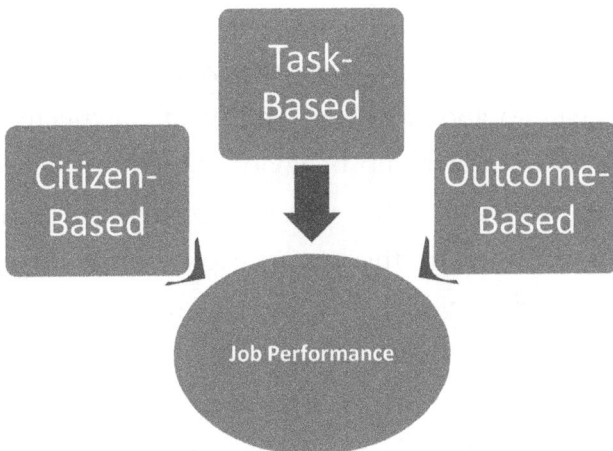

The three broad criteria related to job performance underscore the importance of being a well-rounded employee. The following sections describe these criteria in greater detail.

Citizen-Based Job Performance

An employee's job performance can be assessed based upon his or her relationship with the entire organization. For example, organizations seek employees who will have a positive working relationship with colleagues, customers, and supervisors (also known as internal and external customers). If an employee is known for being dedicated and committed but is unable to get along with his or her peers, then the employee is considered to be more of a liability than an asset. The ideal employee will not only have a positive relationship with his or her peers, but will also promote a positive working relationship when he or she notices counterproductive behaviors. By the same token, organizations seek employees who will promote the organization in public and participate in voluntary meetings. The essence of being an "outstanding" employee has become the norm in many organizations. Most people would agree that employees who are considered to be "outstanding" or "valuable" have more job security and stability. At times, employees will go above and beyond what is expected of them to illustrate their citizenship behavior, which can be defined as voluntary employee activities that may or may not be rewarded and that contribute to the progression of the organization. Being a good citizen in a society (macro level) is similar to being a good citizen in an organization (micro level). Citizens of a society strive to be "outstanding" societal citizens by doing a little extra to help the society develop and citizens of an organization strive to be "outstanding" organizational citizens to help the organization progress. According to Coleman and Borman (2000), there are two main citizenship behaviors that contribute to an organization's success: interpersonal and organizational (as illustrated in Figure 10).

Two Types of Citizenship Behaviors
Figure 10

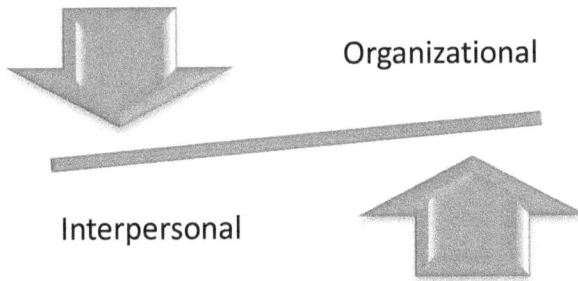

Interpersonal citizenship behaviors involve assisting, supporting, and developing coworkers and colleagues. For example, an employee with high interpersonal citizenship behaviors will attempt to motivate and unite fellow employees who are disengaged from the others. An additional example of interpersonal citizenship behaviors would be an employee who is respectful and courteous to all employees. Some employers acknowledge the importance of mentoring employees who are new to the organization. Kaifi (2011) explains, "The mentoring system is also used in organizations for individuals who are new to the organization" (p. 91). At times, there may be conflicts between employees and those with high interpersonal citizenship behaviors are able to diffuse the conflict before it escalates, which relates to sportsmanship. "Sportsmanship involves maintaining a good attitude with coworkers, even when they've done something annoying or when the unit is going through tough times" (Colquitt, Lepine, & Wesson, 2011, p. 42). One of the most crucial attributes of a person with high interpersonal citizenship behaviors is the ability to understand and appreciate individual differences. "In general, individual differences exert a profound effect on job performance and behavior. Such differences refer to variations in how people respond to the same situation based on personal characteristics" (DuBrin, 2007, p. 17). Thus, it becomes apparent that having interpersonal citizenship behaviors can positively influence job performance.

Organizational citizenship behaviors are just as important as interpersonal citizenship behaviors. These behaviors benefit the larger organization by supporting and defending the company, working to improve its image, and manifesting loyalty. One way this can be achieved is via boosterism. Boosterism is defined as representing the organization in a positive way when in public and away from the office. For example, a person who wears company attire or a uniform in public is directly or indirectly promoting the company and engaging in high levels of boosterism. A different example would be an employee who boasts about his or her company to friends and family. Civic virtue is also a different form of organizational citizenship behavior. Civic virtue refers to participating in a company's operations by volunteering for new responsibilities, attending voluntary meetings and functions, and keeping up to date with information that affects the company. An example of civic virtue is an employee who attends not only his or her own department meetings, but also the meetings of departments that he or she is not affiliated with. Employees who have high levels of organizational citizenship behavior are also known to constructively voice their opinions in meetings as opposed to passively complaining about new policies and procedures when in public. There is definitely a correlation between organizational citizenship behaviors and job performance (Podsakoff, Whiting, Podsakoff, & Blume, 2009; Motowidlo, 2000; Podsakoff, Ahearne, & MacKenzie, 1997; Allen & Rush, 1998).

Task-Based Job Performance

A job description will usually indicate the different tasks for which a potential employee will be responsible. Organizations are known to come up with job descriptions that provide a general standard for interested applicants. Organizations are also notorious for including the following sentence at the end of a job description: *Employee may be asked to perform other duties as required.* This significant sentence legally allows an employer to modify job descriptions at any time and without notice. The Occupational Information Network (or O*NET) is a useful website for learning about different jobs and the tasks associated with each job (www.onetonline.org). The following job description illustrates the tasks for which an Assistant Professor of Marketing is responsible.

Job Description Example
Figure 11

Assistant Professor of Marketing

Responsibilities: Teach general Marketing courses and/or concentration courses as appropriate per academic credentials, advise students, and serve on Department and University committees. The preferred candidates will be able to conduct research in their areas of expertise and/or related fields. Participate in the ongoing development of the curriculum. Continue professional development and scholarship in teaching areas, research and academic writing. Positions require teaching excellence and scholarly productivity. Employee may be asked to perform other duties as required.

It can be concluded from the brief job description above (Figure 11) that a potential employee is responsible for researching (creative), performing other duties as required (adaptive), and teaching (routine) at the university. Indeed, task-based job performance has three general categories: creative, adaptive, and routine. The "CAR" acronym, seen in Figure 12, can be used for recalling the task performance criteria.

Task Performance Criteria
Figure 12

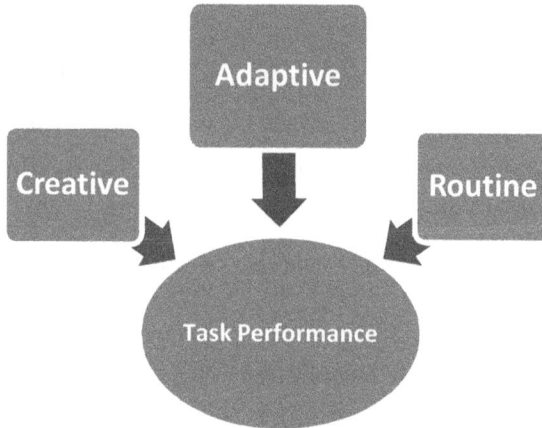

Adaptive

Creative

Routine

Task Performance

Creative task performance is the degree to which employees develop and implement ideas that are both novel and useful. The reality is that creative task performance plays a larger role in all jobs. For example, Google engineers can spend up to 20 percent of their time on a project of their choice because creativity is valued and encouraged by the organization. By the same token, the employees of 3M are allowed to use 15 percent of their time to think creatively. Both companies credit these unique programs as the source of their most successful products. In some professions (e.g., marketing or advertising), creative task performance is considered more important than any other task performance. Furthermore, professors are also encouraged to be creative and publish in prestigious academic journals. Figure 10 illuminated the importance of a professor being able to publish. The classic saying, *"publish or perish,"* holds true in academia. Imagine one-third of a professor's job (or more) being dependent upon his or her ability to be creative and publish novel concepts. With globalization and competition, creative task performance will continue to play a major role in all jobs of the future.

Adaptive task performance requires an employee to be able to *"adapt and overcome"* novel or unusual situations. A case in point is when Chelsey B. Sullenberger, the pilot of US Airways Flight 1549 (January 15, 2009), discovered his plane had lost power and he decided to land in the Hudson River. Captain Sullenberger's heroic actions saved the lives of 150 passengers and crew. A different example (occurred on January 9, 2011) is when U.S. Representative Gabrielle Giffords was shot in Arizona and her aide (Daniel Hernandez Jr., who was only five days into his new job) came to her rescue and performed first-aid. Both examples elucidate adaptive task performances that are novel and unusual. All jobs have a component of adaptive task performance that can be extreme or insignificant.

Routine task performance is associated with being responsible for the same task each day with very minimal variety or change. A classic example of routine task performance would be an employee who works on an automobile assembly line. Each person who works on an automobile assembly line has a very specific job such as screwing on doors or bumpers. This "division of labor" concept is used in many organizations to help enhance productivity levels. For example, contemporary hospitals have been known to request radiologists to specialize and analyze specific digital images (e.g., CT scans, MRI scans, or mammograms) to help productivity, efficiency, accountability, and efficacy levels. In some situations, it makes more sense to divide work amongst a group of employees as opposed to having a group of employees working on the same tasks and doing double-work.

Outcome-Based Job Performance

Outcome-based job performance evaluation is becoming more prevalent because of global competition. Most developed societies have a significant amount of individuals with high levels of education and skills. Interestingly enough, there are about 12,000 colleges and universities in the world, of which, approximately 4,000 are in the US alone (Friedman, 2006, p. 317). With so many educated and dedicated individuals, some organizations believe that the most decisive way to analyze job performance is by evaluating the outcomes that are produced.

Employees can be great organizational citizens who complete all of their tasks in a timely manner; but what about the quality of their work, or the impact of their work on the organization, or the overall value of the employee to the organization? For example, in education, teachers are evaluated based upon the "learning outcomes" of students. If a specific teacher's students are continuously able to perform well on standardized assessments, then the teacher will have more opportunities to teach. This same standard of evaluation of outcomes is also true for attorneys. For example, if a trial lawyer is able to produce exceptional "trial outcomes" by winning a lot of cases, he or she will have more clients and therefore more job security. Figure 13 illustrates the three primary criteria that are relevant to outcome-based job performance.

Outcome-Based Criteria
Figure 13

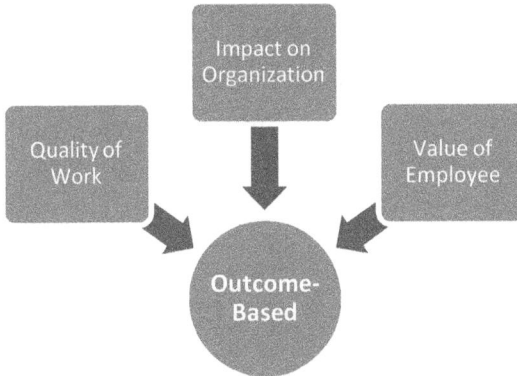

Impact on Organization

Quality of Work

Value of Employee

Outcome-Based

When focusing on outcomes, quality of work determines the impact an employee has on the organization, which in turn, determines an employee's value. Quality of work is becoming more and more important because jobs have changed so much over the years. Starting in the late 1980s, the majority of jobs relied upon conceptual and cognitive work in organizations, (knowledge work), as opposed to the physical and strenuous work in plants and factories (service work). Employees started having free time to think about "creative" products and solutions. The quality of one's work has become a competitive force that filters out sub-optimal employees in many organizations. Employers are notorious for putting employees on a "Performance Improvement Plan" (also known as a PIP) when their quality of work does not meet the organization's standard. Organizations have a specific purpose for existing and therefore, expect employees to complete all of their tasks to meet that purpose. Once the tasks are completed, managers will evaluate the quality of their employee's work and will then make recommendations for continuous improvements. This quality control system has been instilled in the educated workforce for many years. For example, each night students are given homework or tasks to complete; the next day the instructor evaluates the quality of their work, and finally makes recommendations for improvement. In many situations, the quality of one's work is measured by the impact the employee has on the overall organization. For example, certain universities are distinguished for the research endeavors and service of specific faculty members.

Moreover, the impact employees have on an organization is crucial to job performance. A case in point is Stanford University, where faculty members have won over 25 Nobel Prizes in various categories since the university's inception in 1891. The contributions of these individuals have had a tremendous impact on the culture, prestige, and reputation of Stanford University. As an ominously contrasting example, Enron's Board of Directors' decisions to ignore illegal accounting practices led to a historic debacle and bankruptcy. As a direct result, the Sarbanes–Oxley Act of 2002, a federal law that set new standards for all U.S. public company boards, and management and public accounting firms, was created and implemented to stop illegal accounting practices. As these examples have demonstrated, the outcome of employees' job performance can either have a positive or negative impact on the organization. Each employee has a specific value that is a result of his or her overall job performance. Throughout most organizations, it is not uncommon to hear that all employees are "replaceable" or that the organization has an "at-will employment" policy.

Regardless of the situation, employees are constantly evaluated to figure out what quantitative and qualitative value they bring to the organization. It is very common for managers to consider whether or not they can afford to get rid of an employee and hire a new employee or if it is more beneficial to keep an employee who has tenure and value. The reality is that good employees are inimitable and cannot be cloned because they have a unique personality, work ethic, and sense of being. Furthermore, good employees create a history with the leaders of the organization, fellow employees, and customers. This organizational history can never be repeated. Figure 14 illustrates the Job Performance Framework.

Job Performance Framework
Figure 14

Counterproductive Behaviors

Counterproductive behaviors are inevitable in most organizations. These behaviors can be defined as employee behaviors that harm an organization and prevent it from goal achievement. Counterproductive behaviors can be either organizational or interpersonal. These behaviors affect the entire organization in some aspect. Figure 15 below, illustrates some of the behaviors associated with each counterproductive behavior. For example, if an employee is wasting resources, then his or her peers will have fewer resources with which to work.

Examples of Counterproductive Behaviors
Figure 15

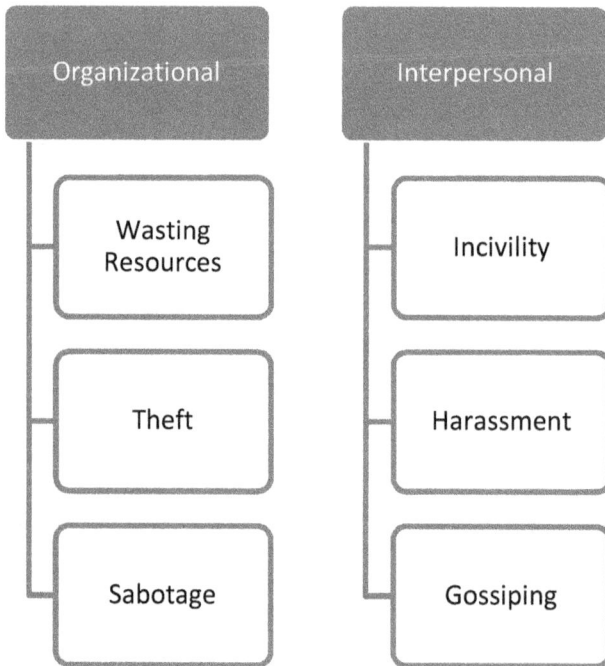

Managers are responsible for dealing with organizational and interpersonal counterproductive behaviors. Many counterproductive behaviors result in immediate termination of the employee, while some counterproductive behaviors result in the employee being formally reprimanded. At some organizations, employee turnover is prevalent, which is why managers focus on recruiting the "right" employees, continuously training employees, and retaining valuable employees who can be developed into competitive advantages. Managers use different performance management tools and plans to assess employees on a regular basis. These techniques are also known as performance appraisals.

Performance Appraisal and Management

The information that emerges from a performance-appraisal can be used by supervisors to manage and develop the performance of employees. By conducting performance appraisals, an organization can strive to reach peak performance levels. Hallowell (2011) states, "What I mean by peak performance—and what most of us seek in our lives and what managers wish to help their people achieve—is consistent excellence with improvement over time at a specific task or set of tasks" and further explains, "Those three factors—excellence, consistency, and ongoing improvement—define peak performance for my purposes" (p. 32). Managers should always be on the lookout for employees who are dissatisfied with their responsibilities. Hallowell (2011) explains, "you can tell if a person is not in the right role if he feels no enthusiasm for what he's doing, if his mind never lights up, if he never gets excited about his job, if he chronically complains" and further explains,

"This doesn't mean he's a dull person or that the line of work he has chosen is intrinsically dull, just that he's not assigned to the right task" (p. 47). Appraisal data can be used to reveal employees' performance strengths and weaknesses. Hallowell (2011) explains, "The goal is for employees to spend as much time as possible at the intersection of three spheres: what they like to do, what they are most skilled at doing, and what adds value to the project or organization" (p. 49). Strategic leaders are known for being able to precisely match skills to tasks. Furthermore, strategic leaders are known for being able to implement effective performance appraisal systems for gauging how employees are performing. Unfortunately, many organizations have reported that their appraisal systems offer little or no value to their organization. According to Bernardin and Russell (1998), "While over 95 percent of organizations report the use of formal systems of appraisal, the majority of those involved in this activity express considerable dissatisfaction with it" (p. 237).

Management by Objectives

Management by Objectives (MBO) is a management philosophy that assesses an employee's overall performance (results) on predetermined goals. When determining the goals, a manager and employee will have a meeting to review the organization's goals and then will determine goals that are specific, measurable, attainable, results-based, and time-sensitive (SMART). Chapter 7 will discuss in depth how SMART goals can be used for motivating employees.

Management by Objectives (MBO) Process
Figure 16

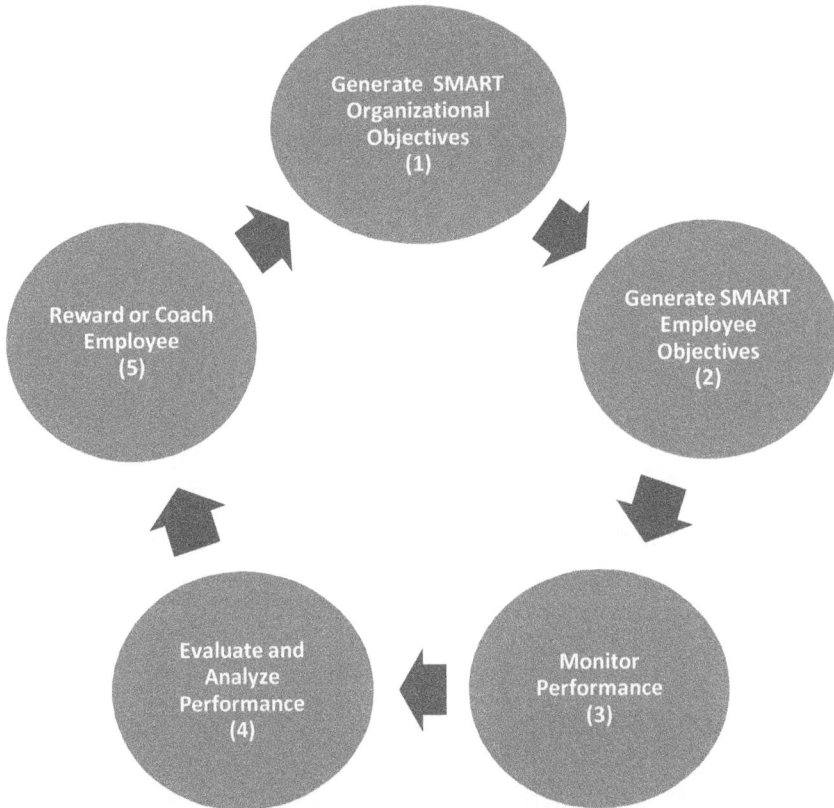

During the review period, progress toward specific goals is monitored by the supervisor. Employees who work for the same department or unit may have several target goals that are similar and several target goals that are specific to each employee. Figure 16 provides an illustration of the MBO process.

Behavioral Anchored Rating Scales

Behaviorally Anchored Rating Scales (BARS) directly assess performance behaviors as opposed to performance results (e.g., MBO). The BARS method depends upon critical incidents or short descriptions of effective and ineffective behaviors that ultimately produce a number value. A manager that uses the BARS approach to assess his or her employees can be compared to an instructor who uses a standardized rubric for grading assignments. Ultimately, the assessor is responsible for rating the specific behaviors of an employee based upon the behavioral expectations that are provided as anchors. When rating the employee, most employers prefer to provide written feedback for why the employee received a specific rating. Colquitt, Lepine, and Wesson (2011) state the following:

> Typically, supervisors rate several performance dimensions using BARS and score an employee's overall job performance by taking the average value across all the dimensions. Because the critical incidents convey the precise kinds of behaviors that are effective and ineffective, feedback from BARS can help an employee develop and improve over time (p. 53).

A manager can use the MBO and BARS approaches (they complement one another) for optimal performance appraisal results. Also, managers can use the overall scores to compare employees. According to Bernardin and Russell (1998), "Thus, the main basis for selecting for selecting a rating instrument should be based on other factors such as how well it fits with the level of precision needed and the purposes to be served by the data (p. 247). Figure 17 provides an example of a simple BARS matrix.

Behavioral Anchored Rating Scales (BARS) Example
Figure 17

Specific Notes	Rating	Meaning	Behavioral Anchors
Reviewed grades w/me on 9/12/2012. Feedback on assignments has helped me develop my writing skills. The lectures keep me engaged.	3	Above Average	My teacher is concerned about my progress toward graduation, provides constructive feedback on assignments, and presents lectures in a logical and concise order.
	2	Average	My teacher is somewhat concerned about my progress toward graduation, provides some constructive feedback on assignments, and presents lectures in a reasonable order.
	1	Below Average	My teacher is not concerned about my progress toward graduation, does not provide feedback on assignments, and does not present lectures in a logical order.

360-Degree Appraisal

The 360-degree appraisal approach entails collecting performance information from several workers who interact with the employee being evaluated. For example, information can be collected from supervisors, subordinates, customers, and peers. In some situations, employees also evaluate their own work as a part of the 360-degree appraisal system. This provides a comprehensive perspective of an employee's performance. Some organizations use the 360-degree appraisal system mainly for developmental purposes because the results can be contradicting. In spite of that possible flaw, the 360-degree appraisal system is a helpful foundational step to learning an employee's strengths and weaknesses and then using that information for generating goals for MBO. Most employees prefer the 360-degree appraisal system because of its comprehensiveness and the amount of information that emerges from multiple sources. Figure 18 offers an example of the different individuals who could potentially evaluate an employee during a 360-degree appraisal.

360-Degree Feedback Example
Figure 18

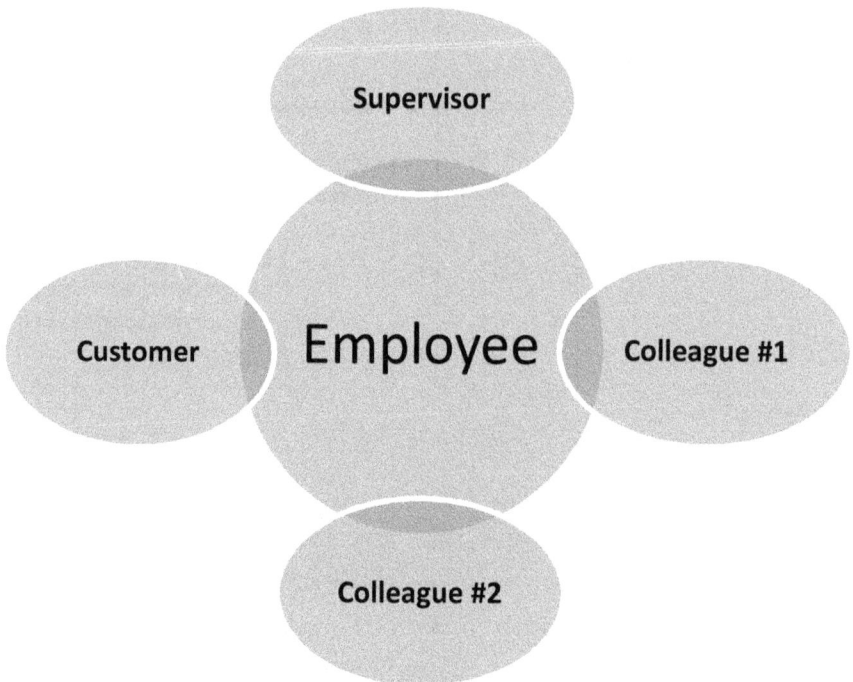

Forced Ranking System

Forced ranking is used by many organizations to evaluate employees based upon job performance. Managers are in charge of ranking the top 10 percent (A players), the vital 80 percent (B players), and the bottom 10 percent (C players). It should be mentioned that Jack Welch (CEO of General Electric from 1981-2001) used a similar ranking system (20%-70%-10%) to make clear distinctions among employees. Contemporary managers prefer to use a (10%-80%-10%) ranking system because only 10% of employees are true "A" players. In most organizations, the vital 80 percent of employees are crucial to the organization's success because the top 10 percent may be overqualified and may consider leaving the organization if a better opportunity arises. Furthermore, the bottom 10 percent of employees can easily be trained or managed out. Thus, it is the vital 80% of employees who are loyal to the organization and depend on the organization for job security and stability. To determine who the A players are, General Electric looks for the employees who have "very high *energy* levels, the ability to *energize* others around common goals, the *edge* to make yes-and-no decisions, and finally the ability to consistently *execute* and deliver on their promises" (Welch, 2001, p. 151). When using specific criteria to evaluate an employee, it becomes imperative to be aware of the halo effect. The halo effect occurs when the rater allows a rating from one dimension to influence the rating on other dimensions. The ranking system puts pressure on the employees (competition) and managers (equitable) to be as unbiased as possible. Some believe the forced ranking system is "inherently unfair because it forces managers to give bad evaluations to employees who may be good performers" (Colquitt, Lepine, & Wesson, 2011, p. 55). Figure 19 provides an example of a forced ranking bell curve.

Forced Ranking Bell Curve
Figure 19

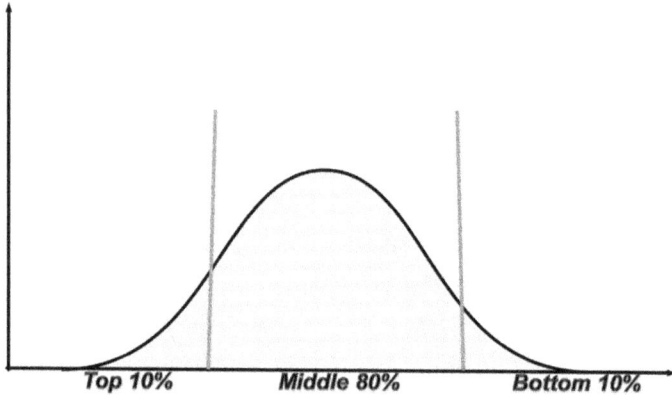

Top 10%   Middle 80%   Bottom 10%

Summary

Chapter 4 discussed the relationship between job performance and citizenship behaviors in the workforce. This chapter also addressed counterproductive behaviors in the workforce. Several performance management tools that can be used for assessing performance were also highlighted in this chapter.

Chapter Review Questions

1. Of the three job performance criteria, which do you think is the most important and why?

2. Why is it important to have both interpersonal and organizational skills in modern day organizations?

3. When researching a job, why is it important to use the Occupational Information Network? What else would you be able to use this site for?

4. Of the three task performance criteria, which do you think is the most important and why?

5. Give three recent examples of adaptive task performances that have been mentioned in the media.

6. Of the three outcomes based criteria, which do you find to be the most important and why?

7. What are some of the strengths and weaknesses with MBO?

8. What are some of the strengths and weaknesses with BARS?

9. What are some of the strengths and weaknesses with the 360-degree appraisal?

10. What are some of the strengths and weaknesses with forced ranking?

Discussion Questions

1. Describe a job in which citizenship behaviors would be especially critical to an organization's strategic goals and one in which citizenship behaviors would be less critical. What is it about a job that makes citizenship more important?

2. If you were the one receiving a 360-degree feedback, whose views would you value the most: your manager's or your peer's? If you were asked to assess a colleague, would you want your opinion to affect that person's upcoming raise or promotion?

3. What is the best combination of performance management appraisals to use? How often should an employee be assessed? If you were asked to create your own performance management instrument, what would it look like?

Case Study

Brian Drummer has been hired as the new manager of the computer department at *Company XYZ*. He has a great work ethic and has many years of experience in sales. *Company XYZ* is known for selling new products as well as used products for a fraction of the price. Many customers appreciate the company's practice of having the option to purchase a used electronic product for a fraction of the price of a new product. More importantly, *Company XYZ* guarantees all new and used products for 90 days. During his second month on the job, Brian tells his sales team that they should no longer sell used products and that he wants his department to be known for only selling new products. His plan was to create a new image for the computer department at *Company XYZ*. Each month his department barely makes their budget for sales but he is proud of the department's new image. He believes that sales will increase with time. Six months into his new position, he is called into the General Manager's office. The General Manager explains to Brian that *Company XYZ* uses a forced ranking system and that he has been ranked in the bottom 10% because of his department's overall performance. Brian is flabbergasted and does not know how to respond. He then hears a knock on the door and the VP of Human Resources enters the office.

Case Questions

1. Conduct a RED Analysis on this case and explain your findings.

2. Who is at fault and why?

3. As the General Manager, what questions (3-5) would you ask Brian Drummer?

4. If you are the VP of HR, how would you handle this situation? Please justify your response.

5. As an outside organizational consultant, what recommendations would you have for the General Manager?

Special Case Assignment

Suppose that the VP of Human Resources went home that evening and created a short survey to hand out to each of Brian's employees the following morning. Her goal is to learn more about Brian's overall job performance.

Create a 10 question survey instrument with a 5-point scale (ranging from strongly disagree to strongly agree) for each question relating to job performance that could be used to yield important data on Brian Drummer for the VP of Human Resources.

5

ORGANIZATIONAL COMMITMENT

Organizational commitment is defined as the aspiration on the part of an employee to remain a member of the organization. Peters, Bhagat, and O'Connor (1981) found that organizational commitment has a stronger relationship with turnover intentions than job satisfaction, even though satisfaction did make an independent contribution to the prediction of turnover intentions. Organizational commitment has been studied in the public, private, and non-profit sector, both nationally and internationally. Hom, Katerburg, and Hulin (1979) compared organizational commitment with facet satisfaction and reported that organizational commitment was a better predictor on intentions to re-enlist in the National Guard. Organizational commitment influences employee retention and turnover levels. How does a manager or leader retain excellent employees? Why are attrition levels so high at so many organizations? Why should employees be loyal to an organization? Jackofsky and Peters (1983) suggested that job turnover should have a strong relationship with job satisfaction whereas organizational turnover should be more highly related to organizational commitment. Voluntary turnover is when an employee decides to leave (quit) the organization and involuntary turnover is when the employer decides to lay-off (downsize/right size) or terminate (fire) an employee. Consequently, when employees leave, it can be quite costly for the organization. For example, if an organization loses an executive, it can cost the organization 4-5 times the annual salary of the executive to replace him or her. Hiring a new employee can be costly because of time spent by HR for recruiting, multiple interviews, relocation costs, training costs, loss of organizational knowledge, overtime pay, decreased morale, and a number of other hidden costs. It is no wonder that organizations continuously survey employees (e.g., employee satisfaction surveys) to determine how employees are feeling about the organization.

Types of Organizational Commitment

There are three types of organizational commitment forces that compel someone to stay in their organization. The three types are: affective commitment, continuance commitment, and normative commitment. Affective commitment is emotion-based. An employee stays at his or her job because he or she wants to. For example, some employees stay at a job because their best friends also work there and it wouldn't feel right if someone left. Continuance commitment is cost-based. An employee stays at his or her job because he or she needs to. Some employees stay at a job because of an upcoming promotion or other financial benefits. Normative commitment is obligation-based. An employee stays at his or her job because he or she feels an obligation not to leave. For example, some employees stay at a job because their direct supervisor invested a significant amount of time training them. Table 3, below offers examples of the three types of organizational commitment.

Three Types of Organizational Commitment
Table 3

Affective Commitment (Emotion-Based)	Continuance Commitment (Cost-Based)	Normative Commitment (Obligation-Based)
Some of my best friends work with me and my job wouldn't be the same if anyone left.	I am close to that promotion for which I have been working so hard.	My direct supervisor has invested a significant amount of time training and mentoring me.
My current position is very rewarding and I look forward to work each day.	As a result of my job, I was able to purchase my dream home in the best part of town.	My company provided me with my first opportunity to work in my field without any experience.
Staying because you *want* to.	**Staying because you *need* to.**	**Staying because you *ought* to.**

Organizations are full of employees with different levels of commitment. Managers are responsible for figuring out how to make the organization a place where employees want to stay, which has a lot to do with the culture of the organization. By creating a dynamic organizational culture, employees will want to stay with the organization.

Survey for Measuring Organizational Commitment

The following survey can be used by managers and leaders to learn more about organizational commitment levels within their organization or department. Employees are asked to indicate the extent of their agreement or disagreement with each statement by circling a number from 1 to 5. A rating of 1 means "Strongly Disagree" and a rating of 5 means "Strongly Agree" regarding each person's attitude toward the organization. Upon completion of the survey, a discussion can take place regarding how organizational commitment levels can be improved. After adding up the numbers for each statement, a total score of 49 or lower indicates low levels of organizational commitment, while a total score of 50 or higher indicates high levels of organizational commitment.

Organizational Commitment Survey
Figure 20

Questions	Scale				
It would be very hard for me to leave my organization right now.	1	2	3	4	5
I do not feel any obligation to remain with my current employer.	1	2	3	4	5
I would be very happy to spend the rest of my career with this organization.	1	2	3	4	5
Even if it were to my advantage, I do not feel it would be right to leave my organization.	1	2	3	4	5
Right now, staying with my department is my desire.	1	2	3	4	5
I feel a strong sense of "belonging" to my department.	1	2	3	4	5
I feel "emotionally attached" to this department.	1	2	3	4	5
I would feel guilty if I left my organization now.	1	2	3	4	5
I feel like "part of the family" in my department because of my friends.	1	2	3	4	5
This organization deserves my loyalty.	1	2	3	4	5
This department has a great deal of personal meaning for me.	1	2	3	4	5
Too much of my life would be disrupted if I decided I wanted to leave my department.	1	2	3	4	5
I owe a great deal to my organization.	1	2	3	4	5
I have a sense of obligation to the people in my organization.	1	2	3	4	5
My life would be disrupted financially if I decided I wanted to leave my department.	1	2	3	4	5
Total Score					

Erosion Model

The erosion model implies that employees with fewer connections or bonds will most likely leave the organization. Thus, this model can help explain why turnover rates are so high in some establishments. It becomes imperative for managers to implement strategies to help employees network within the organization. For example, many organizations are encouraging employees to join customized social networking sites (e.g., www.ning.com or www.yammer.com) to help with this important initiative of building community. Other organizations hold events throughout the year for employees and their families. By implementing such strategies, employees may develop higher levels of affective commitment (emotional ties) to their colleagues and organization. The following image (Figure 21) illustrates a social network diagram.

Social Network Diagram
Figure 21

Although it is beneficial for employees to be well-connected with their peers at work, there can be some unexpected tribulations if employees become attached to one another. The social influence model identifies one main issue that may emerge as a result of this social attachment.

Social Influence Model

The social influence model suggests that employees who have direct connections with "leavers" will most likely leave themselves. Most employees are moderately loyal to their organization and even more loyal to their close colleagues within the organization. If there is a situation where an employee leaves an organization, it is very possible that his or her friends may also leave. The situation becomes contagious and dangerous for the organization. At one university in California, the Dean was forced to resign. As a result, five other managers (Program Chairs) voluntarily left the organization because of their loyalty to the Dean. The college lost a number of key employees along with a significant amount of organizational knowledge. Organizations such as Intel, Publix Super Markets, and Southwest Airlines seem to understand the importance of affective commitment because their voluntary turnover rates (as low as 3%) are significantly less than other well-known organizations. Employees need incentives for staying with an organization. Consequently, it becomes imperative for employers to create a working environment that is unique and hard to leave. As an example, some organizations provide employees with an incentive to telecommute or use flextime. Other organizations have even allowed employees to spend 20% of their time working on personal projects to prevent burn-out from work-related tasks. Furthermore, it has become normal for some larger organizations to provide free lunch for employees, have on-site day care, laundry, fitness centers, and even a mobile medical clinic on-site.

Different Types of Employees

Organizations are full of employees with different skills, expectations, and agendas. Some employees like to "work-the-system" by doing the bare minimum while others work long hours to complete projects in a timely manner. Managers prefer employees with high levels of organizational commitment and task performance. If an employee has high levels of organizational commitment, the employee is more likely to stay with the organization and as a result will help the organization become more effective. In addition, if an employee has high levels of task performance, the employee will be more efficient and productive when working on work-related tasks. Unfortunately, it is very difficult to find employees who have both high levels of task performance and organizational commitment. Griffeth, Gaertner, and Sager (1999) developed a model recognizing the four types of employees: stars, citizens, lone wolves, and apathetics.

Different Types of Employees
Table 4

		Task Performance	
		High	**Low**
Organizational Commitment	**High**	*Stars*	*Citizens*
	Low	*Lone Wolves*	*Apathetics*

As shown in Table 4, stars possess high organizational commitment levels and also high task performance levels. Furthermore, they are recognized as role models. Stars are the employees who are given special tasks to complete, sent to special trainings to represent the organization, are popular within the organization, and are recognized (usually with awards and trophies) at meetings. Citizens possess high organizational commitment levels and low task performance levels. Citizens like to "look busy" by volunteering for extra futile activities such as picking up birthday cakes and taking pictures, showing new employees around, and usually spend a lot of time in the break room. Lone wolves possess low levels of organizational commitment levels but high levels of task performance levels. They have an individualistic agenda of using the organization to achieve their ultimate goal. For example, they use their current job as a "stepping stone" for their next position. They dislike attending meetings or being involved in organizational activities. Apathetics possess low levels of organizational commitment and task performance. Apathetics usually like to "work-the-system" by doing the bare minimum to keep their job; they like to hide in their office and have an excuse for all of their shortcomings. When assigned a task, they like to pass the buck to newer or more dedicated employees. It becomes imperative for managers to be able to recognize who the apathetics of the organization are; they must determine what motivates each apathetic, and then develop an action plan to train or replace that employee.

Withdrawal Behaviors

A classic example of withdrawal behavior is underscored in the movie "*Office Space*" where the main character (Peter Gibbons) clearly demonstrates withdrawal behavior. A memorable scene is when Peter Gibbons has the following shocking dialogue with his occupational hypnotherapist:

Peter Gibbons: So I was sitting in my cubicle today, and I realized, ever since I started working, every single day of my life has been worse than the day before it. So that means that every single day that you see me, that's the worst day of my life.

Dr. Swanson: What about today? Is today the worst day of your life?

Peter Gibbons: Yeah.

Dr. Swanson: Wow, that's messed up.

This comical satire highlights the trials that many employees face on a daily basis. For example, most employees dislike having a number of supervisors to report to, being micro-managed, and dealing with nepotism in the workplace.

Withdrawal behavior is also highlighted in a book entitled *Rivethead: Tales of the Assembly Line*. The book provides a number of examples of how General Motors manufacturing employees took advantage of their organization. For example, one employee confessed, "When it was Bud's turn at the grind, I would hop the line and read paperbacks next to Roy at the worker's picnic bench. It was like being paid to attend the library" (Hamper, 1991, p. 39).

The two types of withdrawal behaviors are psychological withdrawal and physical withdrawal. Psychological withdrawal consists of actions that allow an individual to mentally depart from the work environment. Some examples of psychological withdrawal include: daydreaming, looking busy, moonlighting, and cyberloafing. Physical withdrawal, on the other hand, consists of actions that allow an individual to physically depart from the work environment. Some examples of physical withdrawal are: missing meetings, tardiness, and absenteeism. Employees who appreciate and enjoy the organization where they work are usually punctual, dress up for work, and attend all meetings so they can network with colleagues. At times, when an individual is up for a promotion, other employees will notice the employee dressing up for work (e.g., wearing a tie to work even though it is not required). Consequently, it becomes obvious when an employee becomes disengaged with the organization because of a lack of physical participation. Some employees start coming to work a little late each day, take longer than usual lunch breaks, call-in sick on Fridays and Mondays in order to have a four day weekend, and purposely miss important meetings. In *Office Space*, Peter Gibbons comes to the conclusion that he is sick and tired of work (more specifically, Peter expresses that "there is no motivation for me") and stays home for several days. When he finally returns to work, he dresses more comfortably (very casual) and decides to have a new laissez-faire outlook on his work responsibilities.

Summary

Chapter 5 discussed organizational commitment and included an organizational commitment survey. This chapter addressed the different models that have been used to understand organizational commitment. A number of examples were used to help illustrate key points.

Chapter Review Questions

1. Of the three types of organizational commitment, which do you think is the most important and why?

2. As a manager, how can you improve commitment levels? What would the cost be?

3. How did you score on the organizational commitment level survey? Why do you think you scored the way you did? How often would you prescribe this survey to your employees if you were managing a large organization of 500 employees? Explain why.

4. Do you agree with the erosion model? Justify why.

5. Do you agree with the social influence model? Justify why.

6. What creative strategies would you use to help employees build more connections?

7. As a manager, what strategies would you use to stop the social influence model from happening during lay-offs?

8. As an employee, do you consider yourself a star, citizen, lone wolf, or apathetic? Explain why.

9. What can you do as a manager to help your apathetic employees?

10. As a manager, how would you deal with employees who are guilty of psychological withdrawal? As a manager, how would you deal with employees who are guilty of physical withdrawal? Explain which one is worse. Justify why.

Discussion Questions

1. Describe a job in which organizational commitment would be especially critical to an organization's strategic goals and one in which organizational commitment would be less

critical. What is it about a job that makes commitment more important?

2. How often should a manager gauge employee commitment levels and why? If employee commitment levels are low and voluntary turnover levels are high, how would you address this issue as a manager? Should managers be held responsible for high turnover rates? Justify your response.

3. With organizations becoming more diverse, do you think that organizational commitment levels are going up or down? What kind of impact does the economy have on organizational commitment levels?

Case Study

Jane Johnson is a new manager at *Company XYZ*. After about a month on the job, she realizes that her employees really miss their "old boss" who was promoted to a different position. She understands that she has a difficult job ahead of her. Jane strives to be the best manager she can be; her organizational commitment levels are extremely high and she even comes in on Saturdays to do extra work. After her 90 day probation period is over, she calls a meeting with her middle managers. She makes it very clear that she is upset about the lack of support she is receiving. At one point during the meeting, Jane expressed, "When I walk into the break room, everyone just leaves. I feel like I'm a monster." She is assured by her middle managers that things will come around and that it takes time for staff members to feel comfortable with a new manager; eventually this did prove to be true and her employees became more accepting of her.

Several months later, Jane receives a displeasing phone call from the CEO. She learns that *Company XYZ* will experience some lay-offs and that she will have to lay off at least three of her employees. She will have to figure out which three employees to lay off. Unfortunately, *Company XYZ* did not have a formal way of assessing employee performance. Jane was forced to improvise. Based upon her observations, she decides to lay-off two apathetic employees (Tony and Heather) for not performing up to par and one star (Jacob) because he was too expensive to keep. Soon after the lay-offs take place, Jane notices a significant decline in organizational commitment levels. For example, she notices signs of both physical and psychological withdrawal. Then, without any warning, three of her middle managers (all of whom are stars) storm into her office with letters of resignation. As they leave the building, they tell her she made a big mistake by laying off Jacob. Jane is in complete shock; she does not understand why or how this could happen and calls the Human Resources department. She hears a knock on the door and the VP of Human Resources enters the office.

Case Questions

1. Conduct a RED Analysis on this case and explain your findings.

2. Who is at fault and why? How could this catastrophe have been prevented?

3. As the manager, what questions (3-5) would you ask the VP of Human Resources?

4. If you are the VP of HR, how would you handle this situation? Please justify your response.

5. As an outside organizational consultant, what recommendations would you have for the manager?

Special Case Assignment

Suppose that the VP of Human Resources went home that evening and created a short survey to hand out to each of Jane's employees the following morning. Her goal is to learn about the sudden increase in psychological and physical withdrawals.

Create a 10-question survey instrument with a 5-point scale (ranging from strongly disagree to strongly agree) for each question relating to psychological and physical withdrawal that could be used to yield important data for the VP of Human Resources. Next, draft 5 open-ended questions for the employees to address relating to psychological and physical withdrawal. Finally, create a script that illustrates the dialogue between Jane Johnson and the VP of Human Resources detailing the conclusion of the case study.

6

JOB SATISFACTION

Being in college and declaring a major is an important and strenuous task for students (Kaifi, 2010). Unfortunately, many students make an ill-informed decision about their college major resulting in a career based upon extrinsic values (e.g., salary or social status). After entering the workforce and spending over 2,000 hours a year working, most people realize that there is more to a job than one's salary or social status. Most people start questioning how satisfied they are with their job. Can money really buy happiness? Job satisfaction can be defined as an enjoyable outcome from evaluating one's job or job experiences. Asking students the following question will result in a very interesting discussion: *Would you rather make $75,000 a year and be very happy with your job or make $150,000 a year and hate your job?* Interestingly enough, most undergraduate students with little to no work experience are quick to respond $150,000 a year and when the same question is asked to graduate students with significant work experience, most students are quick to reply $75,000 a year. One way to quickly gauge how you feel about your job is to think about how you feel on a Sunday evening knowing that you have to report to work on Monday morning. If you are excited and happy, then you are probably satisfied with your job and if you are sad and unhappy then you are probably unsatisfied with your job. "Employees with low job satisfaction experience negative feelings when they think about their duties or when they take part in their task activities" (Colquitt, Lepine, & Wesson, 2011, p. 105). As a matter of fact, "workplace surveys suggest that satisfied employees are becoming more and more rare. For example, "one survey showed that just 49 percent of Americans are satisfied with their jobs, down from 58 percent a decade ago" (Koretz, 2003, p. 40). For managers, this is crucial information because there is a correlation between job satisfaction and job performance and also job satisfaction and organizational commitment. Therefore, how can a manger enhance the job satisfaction levels of employees?

Work Values

Job satisfaction depends on what each individual values. In this context, work values can be defined as the things that people consciously or subconsciously desire, aspire to, or want to attain. College graduates should ask themselves what they want from a potential job. Each person will have different expectations or desires and each job will encompass different work values. Some of the commonly assessed work values include: pay, promotions, supervision, coworkers, work itself, altruism, status, and environment (Cable & Edwards, 2004). Which of the work values mentioned above are important to you and why? What are your top three work values? Regardless of your top three work values, you can see that different people value different things and that your values may change during the course of your working life.

Work Values

Table 5

Categories	Specific Values
Pay	*High and stable salary and benefits*
Promotion	*Frequent promotions*
Supervision	*Supervisors from whom you can learn*
Coworker	*Coworkers who you trust*
Work itself	*Autonomy and intellectual stimulation*
Altruism	*Benevolence and goodwill*
Status	*Power and prestige*
Environment	*Safety and comfort*

Pay satisfaction refers to an employee's feelings regarding his or her pay and benefits. A case in point is Starbucks who pays their baristas above minimum wage (plus tips) and provides their full-time and part-time employees with complete health insurance benefits, stock awards, and free coffee. An employee at Starbucks will probably have high levels of pay satisfaction compared to a barista at a different coffee shop.

Promotion satisfaction refers to an employee's feelings about the organization's promotion opportunities. An example is Kaiser Permanente (the nation's largest HMO) which strives to promote from within the organization. It is very common to find employees who have spent 30-40 years at Kaiser Permanente in different roles as a result of being promoted. When forced to hire externally, managers prefer to hire family members or friends of existing "star" employees. Kaiser Permanente is an excellent example of an organization that understands the importance of promotion satisfaction.

Supervision satisfaction refers to an employee's feelings about his or her supervisors. Unfortunately, in most cases supervision satisfaction levels are usually low at most organizations. The most obvious reason for why is because supervisors hold employees accountable for their actions. A case in point is Google which strives to build better bosses through a technique known as Project Oxygen. In Project Oxygen, "the statisticians gathered more than 10,000 observations about managers — across more than 100 variables, from various performance reviews, feedback surveys and other reports. Then they spent time coding the comments in order to look for patterns" (Bryant, 2011). One of the study's major findings was that a boss's technical expertise was less important than being accessible.

Coworker satisfaction refers to an employee's feelings about his or her coworkers. A good illustration is Apple which strives to create an environment that underscores teamwork, synergy, and unity. One employee of Apple explained, "I've met the most impactful people of my life while working for Apple and formed many ongoing friendships" and a former employee of Apple mentioned, "I remember being part of a team that opened a store in 2003. I was surrounded by lots of really smart and talented people. The managers realized this and let us do our thing and we ended up being one of the most successful stores in the country" (Denning, 2012). When employees have high levels of coworker satisfaction, they also have higher levels of affective commitment.

Satisfaction with work itself refers to an employee's feelings about his or her work responsibilities. A good example of "satisfaction with work" is Amazon (Amazon.com, Inc.) which hires employees that understand and value customer service. Consequently, by providing high levels of customer service, customers will continue to purchase online from Amazon.com. Although dealing with customer questions and complaints can be a demanding job, Amazon employees take pleasure in helping out their customers. In fact, all employees (including the CEO Jeff Bezos) spend two days a year answering customer service calls (Green, 2009). This provides all employees an opportunity to not only assist customers but also learn about some of their business shortcomings.

Altruistic satisfaction refers to an employee's feelings about how much of a job entails helping others. An example of an altruistic profession is becoming a police officer. An individual does not become a police officer because of the pay but rather because of the ability to help others. By being able to help others, an individual feels a sense of innate satisfaction that cannot be replaced by extrinsic rewards. Furthermore, many of the jobs in the public sector are connected to altruistic desires.

Status satisfaction refers to an employee's feelings about how one's job is regarded and respected in comparison to other jobs in a society. For example, teachers help mold, educate, and develop a society. Unfortunately, teachers in the Unites States are underpaid and undervalued which explains why the US educational system and test scores (e.g., Program for International Student Assessment) cannot compare with countries like Finland or South Korea. Interestingly enough, the degree of respect and trust teachers are given in Finland can be compared to the status that physicians enjoy in the United States.

Environment satisfaction refers to an employee's feelings about how safe and comfortable a job is. Some jobs are very safe and are inside of a secure building while other jobs are outdoors in a hazardous environment. For example, miners have dangerous jobs. In 2010, approximately 30 miners were trapped underground in Chile for over 65 days. The men were working at a depth of around 2,300 feet at the San Jose mine, near the city of Copiapo, when the rock above them collapsed. Fortunately, the miners were rescued with no casualties. Being satisfied with your work environment is extremely important and should be taken into consideration when accepting a job.

Job satisfaction has several aspects that can be equally as important when reflecting on what a job offers. Consider the following questions: Can money buy happiness? Can a high salary justify an unpleasant work environment? What do you value in a job? Who do you prefer to work with?

Value-Percept Theory

As mentioned above, values influence job satisfaction and different people have different values. Locke (1976) argued that individuals' values would determine what satisfied them on the job. Only the unfulfilled job values that were important to the individual would be dissatisfying. The value-percept theory argues that job satisfaction depends on whether or not one perceives that one's job supplies the things that one values. According to Locke's value-percept theory, job satisfaction can be modeled by the following formula:

$$\text{Dissatisfaction} = (V_{want} - V_{have})(V_{importance})$$

In order to understand the formula, it is important to define each variable.

Definitions of Value-Percept Theory Variables
Table 6

Variable	Meaning
Dissatisfaction	Reflects an unpleasant state of mind
V_{want}	Reflects how much of a value an employee wants
V_{have}	Indicates how much of the value the job supplies
$V_{importance}$	Reflects how important the value is to the employee

As a practical example relating to the value-percept theory and pay satisfaction, a teacher may want an annual salary of $75,000 but may only be earning $60,000 a year. Therefore, there is a $15,000 difference between the teacher's ideal earning and actual earning. Would this difference imply that the teacher is dissatisfied? Not necessarily, for this teacher, satisfaction would depend on whether or not the teacher values pay. If the teacher doesn't value pay, then the teacher will not be dissatisfied in terms of pay. On the other hand, if a physician wants a salary of $500,000 a year and is making $350,000 a year, then that is a difference of $150,000 a year. If the physician values pay then the physician will be dissatisfied. As a practical example relating to promotion satisfaction, an assistant professor may want to become a full professor within five years when the average time can be ten years. This is a difference of five years. If the assistant professor places a high value on promotion, then he or she will be dissatisfied. If the assistant professor does not place a high value on promotion, then he or she will not be dissatisfied. The key variable is how important each value ($V_{importance}$) is to an individual.

Values and Cultural Differences

With globalization and organizations becoming more diverse, it becomes imperative for managers to learn and understand the influence of culture on values. For example, employees in the United States prefer to have rewards allocated according to merit. In contrast, employees in other countries such as Japan, Afghanistan, and Sweden prefer that rewards be allocated equally. Interestingly enough, employees in India prefer allocating rewards based upon need. In many Muslim countries (e.g., Indonesia, Malaysia, Afghanistan, Pakistan, Iran, Sudan, Algeria, Saudi Arabia, etc.) around the world, values such as honesty, humility, accountability, and discipline are influenced by Islam because Muslims believe that Islam is not only a religion but also a complete way of life. Countries such as China and Mexico value a person's contributions to relationships in the work team while the United States and the Netherlands value a person's contributions to task accomplishment. Over the years, managers have used different tools to gauge satisfaction levels.

Job Descriptive Index

One of the most widely used job satisfaction surveys is the Job Description Index (JDI). This survey evaluates the five main satisfaction facets: pay satisfaction, promotion satisfaction, supervisor satisfaction, coworker satisfaction, and satisfaction with work itself. Below is an example of a JDI survey that managers can use to learn more about employee job satisfaction levels.

An Example of a Job Satisfaction Survey
Figure 22

Job Descriptive Index (JDI)		
A.		**Compensation and Benefits Satisfaction**
	3	Above average
	2	Average
	1	Below average
B.		**Promotion Satisfaction**
	3	Above average
	2	Average
	1	Below average
C.		**Supervision Satisfaction**
	3	Above average
	2	Average
	1	Below average
D.		**Co-worker Satisfaction**
	3	Above average
	2	Average
	1	Below average
E.		**Nature of the Work Itself Satisfaction**
	3	Above average
	2	Average
	1	Below average
Total		
Mean		

For optimum results, a manager should attempt to have the majority of his or her employees in the organization take the survey anonymously, once or twice a year. To analyze the data, management can aggregate the numbers to learn about organizational strengths and weaknesses. An aggregated (i.e., mean) score of 2.4 or lower can equate to low job satisfaction levels within the organization. Once the scores are aggregated and made available to all employees, a candid discussion with the employees should take place using the RED Analysis for recognizing the main problems, evaluating the problems, and developing action plans for continuous improvement purposes. Managers should also be aware of how job satisfaction levels fluctuate throughout the day for most employees.

Typical Workday Fluctuations in Job Satisfaction

Most employees have to commute to work in the morning. Once they are at work, they are overwhelmed with emails, phone calls, meetings, and tasks that need to be completed. This ongoing cycle of pandemonium makes it difficult to be satisfied with one's job. The following chart depicts the typical workday fluctuations in job satisfaction for an entry level software engineer. As can be seen, the software engineer is the most satisfied during breaks and the least satisfied during meetings with colleagues. It should be mentioned that most individuals do not actually work eight hour shifts; instead they realistically work four to five hours a day. A significant amount of time is used for taking breaks which includes eating, moonlighting, cyberloafing, socializing, reflecting, and daydreaming. As mentioned above, it becomes imperative for individuals to find a vocation that suits their needs, values, and interests. To help enhance job satisfaction levels, some organizations (e.g., SAS Institute) have an on-site gym with a pool, billiards, volleyball courts, soccer fields, tennis courts, and a putting green. The chart below highlights the workday fluctuations of a software engineer but also resonates with many employees from different professions.

Satisfaction Levels for Typical Workday
Figure 23

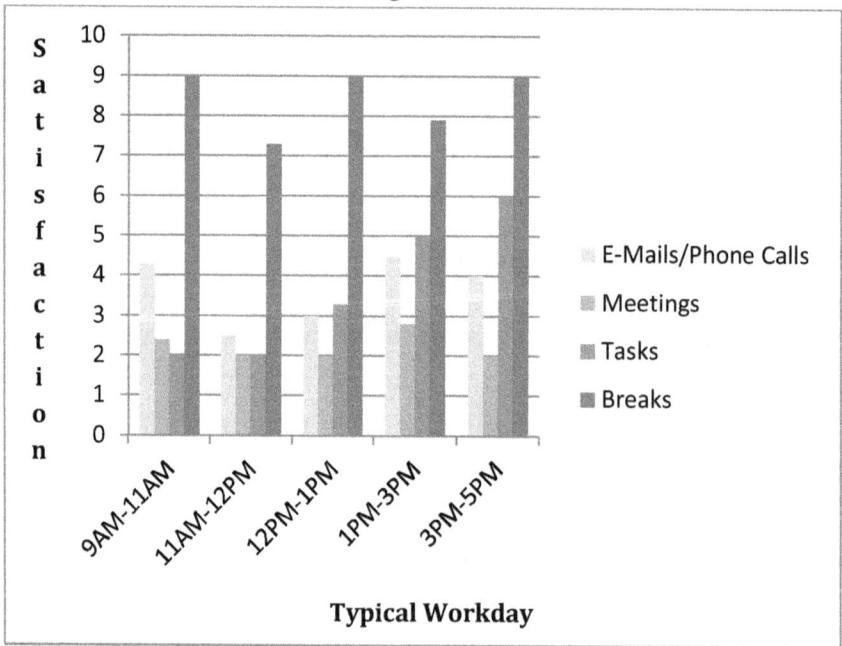

There are a number of reasons for why employees are satisfied or dissatisfied with their jobs. The following chart lists the 10 happiest jobs and the 10 most hated jobs.

The Ten Happiest Jobs and Ten Most Hated Jobs
Table 7

The Ten Happiest Jobs	The Ten Most Hated Jobs
1. *Clergy*: The least worldly are reported to be the happiest of all.	1. Director of Information Technology
2. *Firefighters*: Eighty percent of firefighters are "very satisfied" with their jobs, which involve helping people.	2. Director of Sales and Marketing
3. *Physical therapists*: Social interaction and helping people apparently make this job one of the happiest.	3. Product Manager
4. *Authors*: For most authors, the pay is ridiculously low or non-existent, but the autonomy of writing down the contents of your own mind apparently leads to happiness.	4. Senior Web Developer
5. *Special education teachers*: If you don't care about money, a job as a special education teacher might be a happy profession. The annual salary averages just under $50,000.	5. Technical Specialist
6. *Teachers*: Teachers in general report being happy with their jobs, despite the current issues with education funding and classroom conditions. The profession continues to attract young idealists, although fifty percent of new teachers are gone within five years.	6. Electronics Technician
7. *Artists*: Sculptors and painters report high job satisfaction, despite the great difficulty in making a living from it.	7. Law Clerk
8. *Psychologists*: Psychologists may or may not be able to solve other people's problems, but it seems that they have managed to solve their own.	8. Technical Support Analyst
9. *Financial services sales agents*: Sixty-five percent of financial services sales agents are reported to be happy with their jobs. That could be because some of them are clearing more than $90,000 dollars a year on average for a 40-hour work week in a comfortable office environment.	9. CNC Machinist **Computer Numerical Control (CNC) is a process for machining products using a computer program.

10. **Operating engineers**: Playing with giant toys like bulldozers, front-end loaders, backhoes, scrapers, motor graders, shovels, derricks, large pumps, and air compressors can be fun. With more jobs for operating engineers than qualified applicants, operating engineers report being happy.	10. Marketing Manager
Source: The Ten Happiest Jobs by Steve Denning. Retrieved from http ://www.forbes.com/sites/stevedenning/2011/09/12/the-ten-happiest-jobs/ on September 13, 2012 and the National Organization for Research at the University of Chicago.	

It's interesting to compare the ten happiest jobs with the list of the ten most hated jobs, which are generally much better paying and have higher social status.

Job Satisfaction = Life Satisfaction

A 2010 study out of Radford University in Virginia sheds some interesting light on the divorce rates found within certain professions. People in the workforce with the highest rates of divorce include bartenders, massage therapists, entertainers and performers, choreographers, waiters, nurses, home health aides, and telemarketers whereas occupations with low divorce rates included optometrists, agricultural engineers, clergy, and podiatrists (McCoy & Aamodt, 2010). As mentioned above, it becomes imperative to thoroughly research a profession before starting and selecting a major or entering a career because of the short-term and long-term implications.

Summary

Chapter 6 discussed job satisfaction and the different work values that influence job satisfaction. A survey related to job satisfaction was also highlighted. Professions that typically have high levels of job satisfaction were also addressed. A number of examples were used to help illustrate key points.

Chapter Review Questions

1. Define job satisfaction. Why do you think most employees have low levels of job satisfaction?

2. Define values. Which represent your top five values? Which of these are most important to you and why?

3. Provide a practical example of how supervision satisfaction can be evaluated by using the value-percept theory.

4. Why do you think different cultures have different values? How can a manager satisfy a diverse workforce with different values?

5. Take the Job Descriptive Index (JDI) survey. What is your total score and what is your mean score? Why do you think you have the score that you do? Do you think your colleagues at work would have similar scores? Discuss why or why not.

6. Describe your typical workday and then draw a diagram illustrating your job satisfaction levels throughout the day.

7. Do you agree with the list of the 10 happiest jobs? Explain why.

8. Do you agree with the list of the 10 most hated jobs? Explain why.

9. What are some of the similarities between the 10 happiest jobs?

10. What are some of the links between the 10 most hated jobs list?

Discussion Questions

1. As a future manager, what will you do to enhance promotion satisfaction, supervision satisfaction, and coworker satisfaction at your organization?

2. Do you think there is a correlation between job satisfaction and life satisfaction? Explain why. Do you think there is a correlation between job satisfaction and life expectancy? Explain why.

3. Some organizations have taken creative steps to foster positive satisfaction levels among their employees. For example, there are organizations that have an on-site gym, swimming pool, basketball court, ping-pong tables, and a putting green. Do you think this is a useful tactic? Explain why.

Case Study

Jake Hunter is a manager at *XYZ Radiology* and has been tasked with learning more about job satisfaction levels among his radiologists. The department's recent job satisfaction survey results indicated that 50% of the employees are dissatisfied. Jake's manager believes that the organization should consider making space for a new driving range for the majority of the employees who enjoy playing golf. Jake believes that there might be an easier way to enhance job satisfaction levels among his radiologists. He recalls learning about the Job Satisfaction Theory in college which explains that a job needs the following characteristics in order for the job to be fulfilling and appreciated: variety, identity, significance, autonomy, and feedback. Variety refers to the level of different activities that need to be performed in a job. Upon reflecting on this theory, he realizes that each radiologist is assigned a specific task each day (e.g., analyze CT scans or analyze ultrasounds) and as a result do not have much variety in their job. Identity has to do with completing a job from beginning to end with a visible outcome. The radiologists merely analyze digital images but never meet the actual patients; as a result never know what the actual outcome is for each patient. Significance has to do with the level of impact the job has on people. Although his radiologists have a very demanding job that has a considerable impact on people, some have been anxious about their jobs being outsourced. Autonomy has to do with the level of freedom that the job provides. Jake recognizes that the chief of radiology can be a micro-manager at times. Feedback refers to the level of critique (positive and negative) that is provided to an employee. Jake acknowledges that his radiologists never receive any feedback and are just expected to do their jobs. He feels that he is on to something but is not quite sure. He decides to call his friend who is an "organizational development doctor" to analyze and diagnose his company's ailments.

Case Questions

1. Do you think that creating a driving range for the radiologists is the best solution to the problem or should Jake go with his gut instinct and use the Job Characteristics Theory to evaluate each job (i.e. job analysis)? Explain why.

2. What questions should the organizational development doctor ask the radiologists?

3. If Jake decides to go with his gut instinct, how should he present his proposal to his manager: via email, telephone, one-on-one meeting, or during the next department meeting? Justify your response.

4. Conduct a RED Analysis on this case and explain your findings.

5. How can the work of Robert Owen, Andrew Ure, and Elton Mayo be applied to this case?

Special Case Assignment

Suppose that Jake went home that evening and decided that he needs to survey his employees one more time using a new tool. He calls his "organizational development doctor" friend and learns that the level of unhappiness at some organizations can be captured by an employee satisfaction survey known as the Net Promoter Score (NPS). The key question asks employees to rate, on a scale of 1 to 10, "How likely are you to recommend working at your organization to an interested friend or family member?" Anyone who offers a 9 or 10 is considered a "promoter", while anyone who offers a six or below is considered a "detractor." A score of seven or eight is simply cancelled out.

After doing some research and reflecting, what are the pros and cons to using a Net Promoter Score?

7

MOTIVATION

Motivation is needed to complete a task. The word motivation is derived from the Latin word for movement (i.e., *movere*). Motivation can be defined as a set of energetic forces that originates from both within and outside an individual that initiates task-related effort. Everyone is motivated differently which is why the topic of motivation is so important for both managers and employees. As a practical example, motivation is needed for jobs that require a 50-60 hour work week commitment. At Enterprise Rent-A-Car where employees work long hours, there are opportunities for performance-based bonuses that motivate employees to work harder and longer. As such, many organizations have used creative strategies to motivate their employees. Mary Kay is known for awarding its top sales representatives with a pink Cadillac. Interestingly enough, Chick-fil-A will give considerable gifts to store operators who are able to increase sales each year (McNerney, 1996). Southwest Airlines uses a different strategy for motivating employees to report to work on time and to not call in sick. Southwest employees with no absences or late arrivals over a three-month period receive two free airline tickets from the company. At

Starbucks, part-time baristas who work at least 20 hours a week receive full benefits. The examples above underscore extrinsic motivational forces for employees (e.g., pay, bonuses, perks, and tangible gifts) but many employees also have intrinsic needs such as skill development, knowledge gain, personal expression, and enjoyment. For example, many teachers are intrinsically motivated. Intrinsic motivation can be defined as motivation that is felt when task performance serves as its own reward. Extrinsic motivation refers to motivation that is controlled by some contingency that depends on task performance.

Expectancy Theory

There is a cognitive process involved when making decisions. Expectancy theory describes the cognitive process that employees go through when making choices. There are three specific stages: expectancy, instrumentality, and valence. Expectancy represents the belief that if an individual exerts a high level of effort in a task, the result will be worthwhile. Instrumentality represents the belief that successful performance will result in an outcome. The term "instrumental" implies helping to accomplish something. For example, "he was instrumental in developing many innovative design concepts." Valence reflects the value of the outcome to the individual. Below is a practical example of the cognitive process.

Expectancy: If I study all night for this exam, I can ace my exam tomorrow.

Instrumentality: If I ace my exam, I can get an academic scholarship.

Valence: The value of the scholarship is $5000.00.
                     What should I do? Is the outcome worth it?

Expectancy Theory
Figure 24

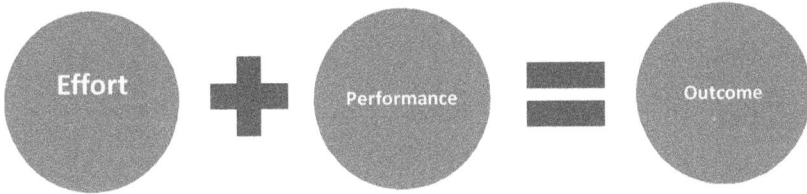

If the value, outcome, or return on investment (ROI) is satisfying, then it is easy to make the right choice and the individual will be highly motivated. In the example above, if the value of the scholarship was only $50.00, then the student will probably be less motivated to stay up all night to study.

Goal Setting Theory

It is important for employees to set goals for themselves on a regular basis. The goal setting theory views goals as the primary drivers for the dedication, discipline, and determination needed to accomplish a task. The theory argues that assigning specific and difficult goals will result in higher levels of performance than assigning no goals, easy goals, or "do your best" goals (Locke & Latham, 1990). It is very common for employees to set goals such as: I would like to be promoted to a management position. The goal is commendable but lacks vital information and is vague. Thus, it is imperative to use SMART goals for optimum results. The acronym SMART stands for: Specific, Measurable, Attainable, Results-based, and Time-sensitive goals. The goal above can be transformed into the following SMART goal: I will become a middle manager making $80,000 a year by September 13, 2013. Organizations are realizing the importance of using SMART goals in all aspects of the workforce (e.g., performance appraisals, implementing policies, forecasting, and financial planning).

Equity Theory

John Stacey Adams, a workplace and behavioral psychologist, developed the concept of equity theory (1963) regarding job motivation. Equity theory acknowledges that motivation doesn't just depend on your own circumstances but also on what happens to other people. Ultimately, it is a measurement of inputs (contributions) and outcomes (rewards). People hold beliefs about their inputs and outcomes. In addition, people form beliefs about others' inputs and outcomes. By comparing ratios based upon perception, an employee can recognize patterns and will be able to determine how to balance equity to support fairness because perceptions of inequity motivate behavior to restore equity. Consider the following scenario:

An NFL football player negotiates a 5-year, $20 million contract. In year 3, the player has a great season and says that he wants to re-negotiate his contract or he will sit out next season.

Why do you think this is happening? The main reason is because the star player believes he has a lot of inputs (contributions) and deserves more outcomes (rewards). He believes that he is bringing a lot to the table when compared to his teammates. Thus, in order for there to be equity, the star player believes he needs a higher salary. Although a high salary may be motivating for some athletes, there is some research that confirms that noncash rewards can be more effective and motivating.

Using Noncash Rewards for Motivation

An article by Jeffrey (2009) was able to show that cash is not always the best incentive for motivation, as would be predicted by economic theory. More specifically, in a laboratory study, working adults who engaged in a challenging mental task performed better in pursuit of a noncash incentive than in pursuit of a cash incentive of equal cash value, even though they stated a preference to receive the cash award. Justification concerns regarding the consumption and purchase of luxurious hedonic goods are found to be a major cause of this behavioral inconsistency. These findings suggest that firms must be very careful when asking employees what incentives they prefer—because the preferred incentive may not be the one that leads to the best performance. Based upon this article's findings, companies like Mary Kay should continue their strategy of awarding the pink Cadillac to their top associates and companies like Enterprise Rent-A-Car should consider adjusting and modifying their monetary bonus programs. In an earlier study, Kovach (1999) explains that managers sometimes disregard the most important motivational techniques when dealing with associates. More specifically, managers often think monetary incentives are the best way to motivate associates, but more often than not nonmonetary incentives are better.

Maslow's Hierarchy of Needs

Psychologist Abraham Maslow's theory of human motivation (1943) emphasizes psychological and interpersonal needs in addition to physical needs and economic necessity. The core of Maslow's theory of human motivation is a hierarchy of five levels of need known as: physiological needs, safety and security needs, belonging (social) needs, self-esteem needs, and self-actualization needs. "Beyond the basics of generous pay, benefits, and time to work on their own personal projects, Google tried to anticipate its employees' needs to save them from wasting time on personal distractions" (Bolman & Deal, 2008, p. 139). Consequently, Google provides medical care, gourmet cafeterias, child care, language classes, self-service laundry, and many other perks that are all free to employees. "With more than 500 applicants for every job opening in 2007, Google was harder to get into than Harvard" (Bolman & Deal, 2008, p. 139). Physiological needs include necessities such as food, water, shelter, and warmth. Safety needs include necessities such as: security, stability, employment, health, and resources. Belonging needs include necessities such as friends, family, and a significant other. Self-esteem needs include necessities such as recognition, respect, confidence, and achievement. Self-actualization needs include necessities such as creativity, pursuing inner talent, morality, and spontaneity. Self-actualization is the highest level in Maslow's hierarchy and focuses on reaching one's full potential. People progress up the hierarchy as they successfully satisfy each need.

Maslow's Hierarchy of Needs
Figure 25

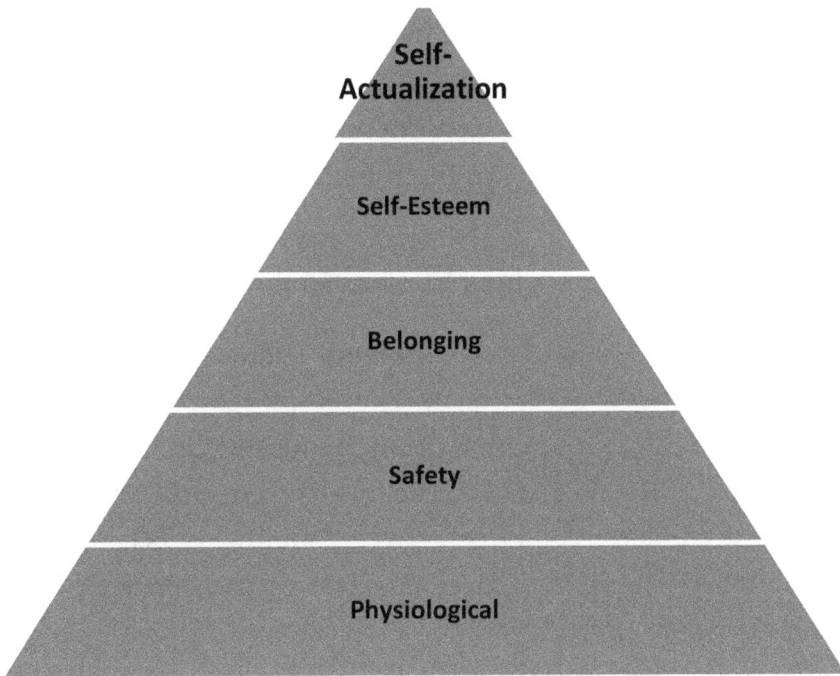

As early as the late 1700s and early 1800s, Robert Owen understood the importance of human needs. At his knitting mill in New Lanark, Scotland, Owen took a new approach:

Owen provided clean, decent housing for his workers and their families in a community free of contagious disease, crime, and gin shops. He took young children out of the factory and enrolled them in a school he founded. There he provided preschool, day care, and a brand of progressive education that stressed learning as a pleasurable experience (along with the first adult night school). The entire business world was shocked when he prohibited corporal punishment in his factory and dumbfounded when he retrained his supervisors in humane disciplinary practices. While offering his workers an extremely high standard of living compared to other workers of the era, Owen was making a fortune at New Lanark. This conundrum drew twenty thousand visitors between 1815 and 1820 (O'Toole, 1995, pp. 201-206).

Applying Maslow's Hierarchy of Needs to Southwest Airlines

Southwest Airlines has a unique culture that is both commendable and exceptional. The employees of Southwest have high levels of organizational commitment levels. Competitors are amazed at the level of dedication, devotion, and loyalty that Southwest Airlines employees have. "Southwest believes that people are willing to work more productively and creatively in an environment that includes humor and laughter" (Colquitt, Lepine, & Wesson, 2011, p. 39). Thus, Southwest values a "fun" environment. Table 8 illustrates how Maslow's Hierarchy of Needs can be applied to Southwest Airlines.

Applying Maslow's Needs Hierarchy
Table 8

Hierarchy of Needs	Southwest Airlines
Physiological	Southwest Airlines emphasis of employees as the airline's "first customers" and passengers as the second has been integral to the organization's success. At the corporate offices of Southwest, employees have been allowed to work in pajamas for a day. Rocking chairs are located throughout the corporate offices for impromptu meetings.

Safety	Southwest Airlines has never had a lay-off. Furthermore, Southwest Airlines is committed to providing their employees a stable work environment with equal opportunity for learning and personal growth.
Belonging	Southwest Airlines stresses training intact work teams in order to build trust among colleagues and also utilizes cross-training in order to facilitate interpersonal helping.
Self-Esteem	Southwest Airlines became the airline industry's most successful firm by hiring people with positive attitudes and well-honed interpersonal skills, including a sense of humor.
Self-Actualization	Southwest Airlines emphasizes an easy-going relaxed corporate style, which provides employees with extensive operational independence. Southwest Airlines was honored as One of the Top 50 Best Places to Work in 2012 by Glassdoor.com. Ranked number ten in the 2012's *list* of *Fortune's World's Most Admired Companies*.
	Sources:http://www.prnewswire.com/news-releases/southwest-airlines-honored-as-one-of-the-top-50-best-places-to-work-in-2012-a-glassdoor-employees-choice-award-135586398.html and http://money.cnn.com/magazines/fortune/most-admired/2012/full_list/

McClelland's Theory of Needs

David McClelland (1961) proposed a theory of motivation that focuses on personality and learned needs. An individual's specific needs are acquired over time and are shaped by one's life experiences. McClelland identified three needs, called manifest needs. These are the needs for achievement, power, and affiliation. These needs are the basis for human motivation and each person has different needs. The need for achievement focuses on: excellence, persistence, and overcoming difficulties. Individuals who are high achievers do a lot of planning and forecasting. The need for power focuses on the desire to influence others and make a difference in life. Individuals with a high need for power like to control people and events. The need for affiliation focuses on establishing relationships with others. Individuals with a high need for affiliation are motivated to express their emotions to others and expect the same in return.

Herzberg's Two Factor Theory

Frederick Herzberg (1950s) expounded on McClelland's theory of motivation and investigated the experiences of satisfied and dissatisfied employees at work, which emerged into a new motivation theory known as the Two-Factor Theory. Herzberg and his colleagues (1959) discovered that people have two sets of needs related to dissatisfaction (avoidance of pain) and satisfaction (related to psychological growth). Thus, conditions at work trigger one of the needs. Work conditions related to satisfaction were labeled motivation factors. Work conditions related to dissatisfaction were labeled hygiene factors.

Hygiene and Motivation Factors
Table 9

Hygiene Factors (Dissatisfaction)	Motivation Factors (Satisfaction)
Company policies	Status and responsibility
Wages and salaries	Opportunity for advancement
Quality of supervision	Gaining recognition
Working conditions	Sense of personal achievement
Feelings of job security	Stimulating work

In order to enhance job satisfaction levels, managers need to focus on building motivation factors into a job. When hygiene factors are poor, there is dissatisfaction among employees.

Reinforcement Theory of Motivation

Psychologist B.F. Skinner (1938) wrote about the reinforcement theory which is one of the oldest theories of motivation. Ultimately, reinforcement theory explains how an individual learns behavior. Reinforcement theory has been used in many areas of study including animal training, raising children, and motivating employees in the workplace. The central premise of the reinforcement theory is to reward an individual for doing a good job, which will result in the individual learning and embracing the behavior.

Theory X and Theory Y

Psychologist Douglas McGregor (1960) developed Theory X and Theory Y modes of management relating to motivation. Supervisors who harbor Theory X assumptions have the pessimistic view that their subordinates are passive and lazy, have little ambition, prefer to be led, and resist change. On the other hand, Theory Y managers embrace an optimistic view and believe that their employees look forward to working and being challenged. Theory Y's key proposition is that "the essential task of management is to arrange organizational conditions so that people can achieve their own goals by directing their efforts toward organizational rewards" (McGregor, 1960, p. 61). These contrasting views play a major role on performance, morale, motivation, and productivity levels. Consider the following table depicting some of the differences between Theory X and Theory Y managers.

Theory X vs. Theory Y
Table 10

Theory X Philosophy	Theory Y Philosophy
Most people dislike working	Most people like working
Most people lack ambition	Most people have significant goals
Most people don't want additional tasks	Most people enjoy additional tasks
Most people are lazy and hate their job	Most people are energetic and enjoy their job
Most people prefer to be led	Most people prefer to lead
Most people work to live	Most people live to work
Most people are gullible and not very bright	Most people are smart and capable
Most people are inherently self-centered	Most people are not inherently self-centered

Contemporary managers agree that the "Theory X and Theory Y" modes of management are both useful and helpful when managing organizations. The point that needs to be emphasized is that managers' assumptions about employees usually become self-fulfilling prophecies. For example, if a manager believes that all of his or her employees are lazy, then that notion will most likely become true. The Theory X perspective is slowly becoming extinct because organizations are continuously evolving (e.g., more skilled and motivated workers). Historically speaking, many employees worked in factories or assembly lines where jobs were broken down into "narrow and repetitive tasks" and today, jobs are more impulsive, mentally robust, and dynamic. By the early 1990s, the majority of new jobs required employees to engage in cognitive work, applying theoretical and analytical knowledge acquired through formal education and continuous learning (Drucker, 1994). This type of work, also called "knowledge work" is becoming more prevalent in many societies. Reich (2002) explains that, "jobs in the old mass-production economy came in a few varieties (research, production, sales, clerical, managerial, professional), but this system has fragmented" (p. 71). As organizations continue to evolve, it becomes imperative for managers to empower, challenge, and motivate employees at all times because the workforce is full of highly skilled and educated individuals who "live to work" in this developed society.

Summary

Chapter 7 discussed a number of motivational theories. This chapter also addressed the importance of using non-cash incentives to motivate employees. A number of examples were used to help illustrate key points.

Chapter Review Questions

1. Define motivation. How should employees be motivated?

2. Do you agree that teachers are intrinsically motivated? Justify your response.

3. Provide an example of the expectancy theory and how it applies to your life.

4. Provide an example of a SMART goal that applies to your life.

5. Do you agree with the equity theory? Justify your response.

6. Do you think non-cash rewards are more effective than cash rewards when motivating an individual? Which do you prefer and why?

7. How would you critique Maslow's Hierarchy of Needs?

8. Why do you think the majority of the motivational theories were created by psychologists and not managers?

9. Do you agree with McClelland's Need Theory? Explain why.

10. Do you prefer a Theory X or Theory Y style of management? Explain why.

Discussion Questions

1. If your manager has a Theory X style of management and you prefer a Theory Y style, how would you deal with the situation?

2. Based upon the different motivational theories discussed throughout this chapter, which theory is the most interesting? Which theory resonates with you the most? As a future manager, how will you motivate your employees?

3. Apply Maslow's Hierarchy of Needs to an organization with which you are familiar. Explain your results.

Case Study

Ashley is a manager at *XYZ Telemarketing*, and has noticed a stark decline in motivation and engagement the last couple of days among her telemarketing staff. She decides to have a meeting with her staff in an attempt to figure out why motivation levels have gone down. At the meeting, Ashley discovers that her telemarketers are not too excited about cash bonuses, there is no job security, and they feel overworked because they don't have any breaks. One senior telemarketer also pointed out that the telemarketers are just expected to work and do not have any daily goals (indirectly stating that the cash bonuses are not connected to performance and are actually connected to favoritism). A different telemarketer explained that her colleagues are "on the phone for long periods of time and do not have access to water" and goes on to say that "the telemarketers are not given any respect and are looked down upon" by upper management. A telemarketer in the back of the room explained, "We are treated as if we are stupid and some of us work harder than others." Ashley is troubled after hearing all of this information and politely says that she will have a follow-up meeting with the staff in three days to discuss their concerns. As Ashley returns to her office, she decides to call her friend who is an "organizational development doctor" to analyze and diagnose her company's ailments.

Case Questions

1. Do you think that a Theory X or Theory Y management style is being used at XYZ Telemarketing? Explain why and provide examples.

2. What questions should the organizational development doctor ask the telemarketers? What questions should the organizational development doctor ask Ashley?

3. What theories can be applied to this case? Explain why and provide examples.

4. Conduct a RED Analysis on this case and explain your findings.

5. How can the work of Robert Owen, Andrew Ure, and Elton Mayo be applied to this case?

Special Case Assignment

Prepare a 10-minute presentation explaining how you would address the issues mentioned in this case. Please make sure to use the theories mentioned in this chapter to help you with your task. Your presentation is what Ashley will use in her follow-up meeting with her telemarketing staff.

8

ORGANIZATIONAL CULTURE

Organizations have their own culture, language, and symbols. Organizational culture can be defined as the values and behaviors that contribute to the unique environment of an organization. An organization's culture is the DNA of an organization. Thus, each organization has its own culture that cannot necessarily be imitated because the personnel create the culture of the organization. An organization's culture can even influence the hiring process. For example, Jeffrey Swartz, CEO of Timberland, has an interesting way of hiring employees. Senior applicants go through a day of community service with Timberland's executives because Swartz claims that anyone can be smarter than him during an interview, but service brings out the real person and this is who they try to hire (Xenikou & Simosi, 2006). As a different example, at NetApp, recruiting is done to attract highly altruistic and talented people. Furthermore, NetApp is known for its egalitarian culture. NetApp provides exciting work, flexible scheduling for work-life balance and encourages volunteer efforts in the community. As a matter of fact, NetApp provides "five paid days for volunteer work, $11,390 adoption aid, and autism coverage -- used by 43 employees since 2006 at a cost of $242,452" (Levering & Moskowitz, 2009). BMW also has an exclusive culture. BMW has worked hard to create a culture of innovation in which there is never a penalty for proposing new and outlandish ways of improving cars (Edmondson, 2006). At BMW's Leipzig facility in Germany, the assembly line moves above employee offices to encourage employees to continuously innovate and think of ways of improving the BMW vehicles. At Saturn's Tennessee assembly plant, each car traveled down the assembly line with the customer's name attached to it. Furthermore, there was a ceremony when the customer was handed over the keys resulting in extremely loyal customers (McKnight, Phillips, & Hardgrave, 2009). Edgar Schein, a scholar of organizational culture suggests that an organization's culture has three distinct levels: artifacts, core values, and underlying assumptions.

Artifacts

Every organization has artifacts or symbols that symbolize a specific meaning. Artifacts can be defined as expressions of an organization's culture that employees can easily see or talk about. For example, FedEx's logo has an arrow in between the "E" and the "x" symbolizing moving forward or progressing. What might the symbol convey about the organization's culture?

FedEx Logo
Figure 26

Physical structures also speak volumes about an organization's culture. For example, what is the difference between having rectangular tables versus circular tables or personal offices versus cubicles? Organizations also have their own language that is used among the employees. For example, professors and universities are obsessed with SLO or AoL initiatives. Most people do not know that SLO stands for student learning outcomes and AoL stands for assurance of learning. Rituals are also very common at many organizations. For example, at many retail stores, it is very common to have a cheer in the morning to motivate employees to reach all of their goals for the day.

Stories are also used as a medium for repeating an organization's culture to all employees. As a classic example, Nordstrom employees all know about the importance of customer service but imagine hearing the following story for the first time, "a Nordie once refunded a customer's payment for a set of automobile tires, even though the company had never stocked tires" (Spector & McCarthy, 1995, p. 27). The story allows an employee to visualize, understand, and appreciate the importance of customer service. Organizations have also used success stories of how lower-level employees were able to rise to the top of an organization as a way to orient new employees to an organization's culture. Hiring and promoting from within shows that an organization values loyalty and commitment.

Ceremonies are the formal events that take place in an organization. Most organizations have town hall meetings on a regular basis where the CEO addresses the launch of a new product, new company goals, or even "burn an employee-despised 800-page policy manual" which happened at Continental Airlines (Higgins & McCallaster, 2004). All of these are examples of the use of various artifacts by organizations to express their specific culture.

Core Values

Organizations have core values that shape the culture of the organization. Core values can be defined as the beliefs, philosophies, and norms of an organization that are promoted to all. Whole Foods does an outstanding job of promoting their values. Whole Foods mentions the following on their website, "What's truly important to us as an organization—the following list of core values reflects what is truly important to us as an organization. These are not values that change from time to time, situation to situation or person to person, but rather they are the underpinning of our company culture."

Whole Foods Core Values
Table 11

Whole Foods
1. Selling the highest-quality natural and organic products available.
2. Satisfying and delighting our customers.
3. Supporting team member happiness and excellence.
4. Creating wealth through profits and growth.
5. Caring about our communities and our environment.
6. Creating ongoing win-win partnerships with our suppliers.
7. Promoting the health of our stakeholders through healthy-eating education.
Source: Retrieved from http://www.wholefoodsmarket.com/mission-values/core-values on October 2, 2012.

Underlying Assumptions

Organizations have assumptions that guide behavior. Underlying assumptions can be defined as deeply held beliefs that tell members of an organization how to think about things. As a practical example, in the field of healthcare, it would be unimaginable to deliberately treat a patient with unsterile equipment. Underlying assumptions are the essence of culture and are ingrained in each employee. "They are so strongly held that a member behaving in any fashion that would violate them would be unthinkable. Another characteristic of assumptions is that they are often unconscious. Organization members may not be aware of their assumptions and may be reluctant or unable to discuss them or change them" (Nelson & Quick, 2011, p. 561). The following table provides some examples of assumptions relating to different occupations.

Occupations and Their Underlying Assumptions
Table 12

Occupation	Underlying Assumption
Engineer	Safety
Teacher	Educate
Police Officer	Enforce laws

Southwest Airlines' People Oriented Culture

Imagine working for an organization that has never had a lay-off and where employees are encouraged to express their individuality. Imagine being a part of a culture that deemphasizes both hierarchy and elitism. Furthermore, titles are not important and if an employee has a great idea, it is recommended that the employee go straight to the department head to share that idea. This organization is Southwest Airlines. As a matter of fact, Southwest Airlines defines its culture as "a warrior spirit, leading with a servant's heart, and a fun-loving attitude" (McGee-Cooper, Trammell, & Looper, 2008, p. 49). At this exceptional organization, 120 employees volunteer their time dedicated to a Culture Committee ensuring the company does "whatever it takes to create, enhance, and enrich the special Southwest Spirit and Culture that has made this such a wonderful Company/Family" (McGee-Cooper, Trammell, & Looper, 2008, p. 49).

Southwest Airlines has a commendable organizational culture that truly values its employees. According to the current CEO, Gary Kelly, "Our people are our single greatest strength and most enduring long term competitive advantage." As a result of this dedication to its most important asset, employees at this organization have high levels of organizational commitment and job performance. "One reason that companies like Southwest Airlines are so successful is that they have dedicated employees whose efforts surpass what is formally required of them" (Bolino & Turnley, 2003, p. 60). Gary Kelly mentioned that the difference between his company and others is simple: "People working together, people loving each other, people respecting each other." At this organization, employees are happy and employees respect upper management. Moreover, this progressive organization emphasizes employees as the airline's "first customers" and passengers as the second, which has been integral to the organization's success.

Southwest Airlines has used a unique style for hiring employees. The organization became the airline industry's most successful firm by hiring people with positive attitudes and well-honed interpersonal skills, including a sense of humor. When a group of pilots applying for jobs at Southwest were asked to change into Bermuda shorts for the interviews, two declined. As a result, they weren't hired (Freiberg & Freiberg, 1998). At this organization, it is important to not take yourself too seriously, maintain perspective (balance), celebrate success, enjoy your work, and be a passionate team-player. The former CEO, Herbert "Herb" Kelleher, exemplified this philosophy to the fullest. On Easter, he walked a plane's aisle clad in an Easter bunny outfit, and for St. Patrick's Day he dressed as a leprechaun. When Southwest Airlines started a new route to Sacramento, Kelleher sang a rap song at a press conference with two people in Teenage Mutant Ninja costumes and two others dressed as tomatoes (Levering & Moskowitz, 1993, p. 413).

Southwest Airlines is known for promoting fairness. For example, Southwest's CEO received less than $1 million in 2006 even as the carrier posted its 34th straight year of profits (Roberts, 2007). It should be mentioned that many CEOs of large organizations make over $50 million per year. As a side note, Whole Foods Markets has had a policy limiting executives' pay to ten times the average salary of employers. As a result of having such a unique culture, Southwest Airlines was ranked number ten (2012) in the list of *Fortune's World's Most Admired Companies* and was also honored as *One of the Top 50 Best Places to Work* (2012) by Glassdoor.com.

Nordstrom's Customer Service Culture

Nordstrom department stores (named after John Nordstrom) are renowned for customer service. They have a unique philosophy:

the customer is always right. This culture of high-quality service has become popular in many other industries (e.g., education, entertainment, and food industries). In order to promote such a unique philosophy, employees learn about the values of the organization during the initial employee orientation. "For many years, they were given a 5" x 8" card labeled the "Nordstrom Employee Handbook," which listed only one rule: Use your sound judgment in all situations. Although some changes have been made, the emphasis on customer service is still dominant" (Bolman & Deal, 2008, p. 276). After the orientation, the company relies on acculturated "Nordies" to induct new employees (Bolman & Deal, 2008, p. 275). Like many other organizations, Nordstrom relies on artifacts and has its own unique language. A person who does not work for Nordstrom would never know that "Nordies" are acculturated employees. Furthermore, Nordstrom's physical structure has more seating, better lighting, larger fitting rooms, and wider aisles when compared to other department stores. When inducting new employees, Nordies share stories that consist of anecdotes and legends that are passed down from one cohort to another within an organization. For example, as an employee of Nordstrom, suppose you overheard the following stories during your lunch break:

> A customer fell in love with a particular pair of pleated burgundy slacks on sale at Nordstrom's downtown Seattle store. Unfortunately, the store was out of her size. The sales associate got cash from the department manager, marched across the street, bought the slacks at full price from a competitor, brought them back, and sold them to the customer at Nordstrom's reduced price (Spector & McCarthy, 1995, p. 26).

When a customer inadvertently left her airline ticket on a Nordstrom counter, the sales associate called the airline. When that didn't work, she hopped in a cab, headed for the airport, and handed the ticket to a thankful customer (Spector & McCarthy, 1995, p. 125).

According to legend, a Nordie once refunded a customer's payment for a set of automobile tires, even though the company had never stocked tires. In 1975, Nordstrom had acquired three stores from Northern Commercial in Alaska. The customer had purchased the tires from Northern Commercial, so Nordstrom took them back—as the story goes (Spector & McCarthy, 1995, p. 27).

These stories provide influential social knowledge about the organization's culture and more specifically, the basic underlying assumptions of Nordstrom department stores. The emphasis on customer service is so great that there are monthly store "pow-wows" where customer letters of appreciation are read over the intercom and letters of complaint are also read over the intercom (not mentioning any names). This helps with continuous improvement efforts (Spector & McCarthy, 1995, p. 120-129). Periodic ceremonies such as summer picnics and Christmas dance parties are also opportunities for Nordstrom managers to discuss customer service initiatives. The following table represents Nordstrom's cultural values.

Nordstrom's Cultural Values
Table 13

Nordstrom's Department Stores	
Use good judgment.	We trust each other's integrity and ability. Our only rule: Use good judgment in all situations.
Be empowered.	Want to go above and beyond for a customer? Make a suggestion? Try something new? We want you to take the initiative, and we'll support your efforts to deliver exceptional service.
Setting goals matters.	And we set our goals high. At Nordstrom, you can determine your own success and make a real difference by accomplishing the goals you set.
It's your business.	Our employees have a personal, financial and professional stake in the success of our company. Here, you're encouraged to take ownership of your career.
Healthy competition is good.	We love to win. If you thrive in a high-energy, competitive team environment, you'll love it here.
Be honest.	We value open, honest and respectful communication.
Be recognized.	We value people who drive results, and we regularly recognize outstanding performance — whether you're serving customers or supporting those who do.
Be a good neighbor.	Our company and our employees support hundreds of community organizations through contributions, outreach programs, special events and volunteering their time.
Be kind.	We still believe the golden rule has a lot of merit: Treat others as you'd like to be treated. We work hard to offer great service to each and every customer and we believe great service begins with showing courtesy to everyone, customers and coworkers alike.
Have fun.	Fashion is one of the truest forms of self-expression. It's creative and colorful and totally limitless. If you're passionate about fashion, this is the place for you.
Our door is always open.	Have an idea? Want to talk? If it's important to you, we're listening. It's important to us that every person who works here feels valued, welcome and cared for. And if you've got a great idea, we want to hear about it.
Source: Retrieved from http://www.glassdoor.com/Overview/Working-at-Nordstrom-EI_IE1704.11,20.htm on September 12, 2012.	

The Organizational Culture Profile (OCP)

The Organizational Culture Profile (OCP) was developed by O'Reilly, Chatman, and Caldwell (1991). The OCP has eight dimensions: innovation, attention to detail, outcome orientation, aggressiveness, supportiveness, emphasis on rewards, team orientation, and decisiveness. Originally the OCP was developed to examine the parallel between individual and organizational congruence when evaluating and hiring job applicants. The original version of the OCP consisted of a number of value statements to establish congruency. The OCP can be used to analyze an organization's culture. Organizational consultants, entrepreneurs, researchers, leaders, and managers use the OCP for analyzing and diagnosing organizations. The figure below illustrates the OCP dimensions.

Organizational Culture Profile

Figure 27

Attraction-Selection-Attrition (ASA) Framework

Like human beings, organizations have a unique personality. The Attraction-Selection-Attrition framework explains that potential employees will be attracted to organizations whose cultures match their own personality (Schneider, Goldstein, & Smith, 1995). Ultimately, there needs to be a match between the employee and the organization and also a match between the organization and the employee. As mentioned above, Southwest Airlines became the airline industry's most successful firm by hiring people with positive attitudes and well-honed interpersonal skills, including a sense of humor. At Timberland, senior applicants go through a day of community service with executives. People who do not fit with the organization will be unhappy which will lead to attrition. As a result, it is better to "filter out" the misfits before they are hired.

Subcultures and Countercultures

In many large organizations, it is normal for subcultures to emerge because of strong leaders who are able to influence a group of employees. The people in a subculture usually have their own language, stories, rituals, and ceremonies. For example, a marketing department of an organization may have its own subculture. Most organizations do not mind subcultures as long as they do not interfere with the organization's mission, values, and goals. However, if the values of a subculture interfere with the organization's culture, then it is considered a counterculture. Countercultures can be considered dangerous because they challenge the values of the organization resulting in unhealthy organizational politics.

Summary

Chapter 8 discussed organizational culture and the organizational culture profile. Furthermore, this chapter underscored the organizational cultures of two commendable organizations. A number of examples were used to help illustrate key points.

Chapter Review Questions

1. Define organizational culture. Describe your organization's or university's culture.

2. Conduct some online research and find a logo with a hidden message. Explain what the hidden message is and how it relates to the organization's culture.

3. If you had your own accounting company, what would your seven core values be? Explain why.

4. Think of three different professions and then figure out the underlying assumption for each profession.

5. Do you think that Southwest Airline's people-oriented culture is sustainable? Justify your response.

6. Do you think that Nordstrom's customer service culture is sustainable? Justify your response.

7. Use the Organizational Culture Profile to analyze an organization with which you are familiar. Explain your findings.

8. Do you agree with the ASA framework? Justify your response. As a manager, how will you screen potential employees for organizational fit?

9. As a manager, would you encourage the creation of subcultures? Justify your response.

10. As a manager, how will you eliminate counter cultures?

Discussion Questions

1. In 1994, Denny's settled a discrimination lawsuit. As a result, the company has worked hard to recover from the lawsuit. What are the benefits of fostering a diversity culture?

2. As a future manager, how will you conduct newcomer orientations? What needs to be addressed in the orientations? Who should be present for the orientations? How long should the orientation be? Next, create an agenda for the orientations.

3. If an employee is a good fit for an organization, do you think he or she will have higher job performance levels or organizational commitment levels? Justify your response.

Case Study

Mikey Johnson is a manager at *XYZ Technology* and has recently learned that his company will be merging with *ABC Technology*. He is very excited about the merger because *ABC Technology* is a larger organization with more resources. Mikey feels that *XYZ Technology* is too small and will eventually go bankrupt if it does not merge with a well-known company. *XYZ Technology* has a total of 20 employees, no formal rules, and a culture based upon creativity. As an example, employees are allowed to use 30 percent of their time working on projects of their own choice. Employees are encouraged to work from home as long they complete their work. *XYZ Technology* understands the importance of work/life balance.

A couple of months later, Mikey and his team realize that they are not as happy as they thought they would be after the merger. *ABC Technology* has a different culture than what they are used to. They are no longer allowed to work from home or use 30 percent of their time to work on projects of their own choice. Mikey is also noticing a counterculture forming among his employees. *ABC Technology* expects employees to work six days a week and there is a lot of micro-managing. Mikey is confused and upset; he decides to have a conversation with Arnold, his new supervisor from *ABC Technology*. Mikey learns that things will probably not be changing but he can propose a plan at their next meeting. Mikey goes back into his office and decides to call his friend who is an "organizational development doctor" to analyze and diagnose this situation.

Case Questions

1. What questions should the organizational development doctor ask Mikey? What questions should be asked of Arnold?

2. How should Mikey deal with the clash of cultures?

3. Who is at fault (Mikey or Arnold) and why?

4. What can *ABC Technology* learn from Southwest Airlines?

5. Conduct a RED Analysis on this case and explain your findings.

6. How can the work of Robert Owen, Andrew Ure, and Mary Parker Follett be applied to this case?

Special Case Assignment

Create a 10-minute presentation explaining how you would address the issues mentioned in this case. Please be creative and figure out how you can propose a win-win solution. Your presentation is what Mikey will use in his follow-up meeting with Arnold.

9

INTERVIEWS WITH MANAGERS

Most people would agree that managers have their own way of managing people and understanding organizations. Therefore, it is important to learn from managers based upon their vast experiences. This chapter contains ten interviews with managers from all over the United States. Ellen Herda (1999), an anthropologist and professor at the University of San Francisco, explained, "For every conversation there is a common language or there is the creation of a common language among interlocutors" (p. 121). Each participant provides valuable insights based upon their own experiences. This method of qualitative research can be more effective than surveying 100 managers (i.e., quantitative research method) because in this context the managers are able to elaborate on their responses as oppose to simply selecting a numerical value representing a perspective, feeling, or level of understanding. The managers who were interviewed for this chapter come from different generations and have different perspectives on organizational behavior issues.

Topics relating to leadership style, glass ceiling phenomenon, motivation, performance management system, organizational politics, rewarding employees, and teamwork are discussed in the interviews. It is important to mention that all of the participants have a graduate level degree and significant management experience. The same questions were asked of each participant so it would be more convenient to compare and contrast responses based upon:

- Gender,
- Generational affiliation,
- Management experience,
- Span of control, and
- Other important variables.

At the end of each interview, there is a designated area for taking notes.

It should also be mentioned that many academic journals have sections dedicated to executive interviews because of the knowledge that can be attained from each interview. A case in point is the *Journal of Applied Management and Entrepreneurship* (JAME) that is published out of Nova Southeastern University. Two exceptional executive interviews relating to leadership and organizational behavior that were published in the JAME journal are: "Critical Concepts Applied to Leadership in Energy and Environmental Design: Insights from Karen Maggio" by Kaifi and Do (2012) and "Strategic Leadership Applied to Retail Management: Joe Contrucci Discusses the 21st Century Dynamic Workforce" by Kaifi and Mendenhall (2012).

Laura Bailey is from Generation X and has seven years of management experience in Higher Education.

BK: Should leaders be more task or relationship oriented?

LB: I think they should have a balance between a task-oriented approach and a relationship-oriented approach. Focusing mainly on tasks will eventually create problems with employee motivation. After all, we are not robots. Also, any type of social context involves socialization and relationship-building.

BK: Based on your observations, is there still a glass ceiling in the workforce?

LB: I definitely think there is a glass ceiling for women and minorities in becoming a top-level manager. It is less in the US relatively speaking, but it is still in existence.

BK: Based on your experiences, what is the best way to manage the different generations in the workforce?

LB: I don't really differentiate based on age. I guess because of my cultural background though, I am more patient and understanding with older people.

BK: What generation are you from? What generation/category do the majority of your employees fall under? Has this caused any problems?

LB: I fall under Generation X. A lot of them are older than me. It sometimes becomes an issue that I am younger than them, but I find a way to win people's hearts and minds through kindness and genuine interest in their lives. I think the most important issues stem from the fact that I am from a different nationality.

BK: As a manager, how do you enhance motivation levels? Please provide some examples/stories.

LB: I try to motivate people by connecting with them, building strong relationships, and giving positive feedback. I always place positive feedback first and then I add the issues, if there are any. For instance, asking about how their families are doing can make them feel more like a part of the group and they feel more motivated to help out. Also, an equal environment at work will keep people more motivated. Any type of inequality may cause resentment and decrease motivation.

BK: What skills/traits do leaders need? How can a person develop his or her leadership skills?

LB: Leaders need to display exemplary behavior. There needs to be no conflict between what they practice and what they say. They need to focus on identifying what keeps the staff motivated. Each person is different. Keeping positive and clarifying goals by repeating them in different ways in front of staff can contribute to success. Leaders need to display a passion for their job and communicate to the staff that they are all equal and everybody will be ready to tackle every problem at work. Another good aspect of effective leaders is oratory skills and being good at the art of persuasion. The same idea can be presented by two different people with two different styles and the person who is good at influencing the masses will gain more followers.

BK: Who is a leader that you admire and why? How has this person influenced your leadership style?

LB: A good leader that I admire is a Dean that I work for. He is very smart and has perfect self-discipline. Through his exemplary behaviors, he sets a good example for everybody. Our Associate Dean is also a great leader. He is very humble and he is ready to even vacuum his own office if necessary. He does not expect any special treatment. We all respect him.

BK: Based on your experiences, how has the workforce changed over the years?

LB: The workforce is much more diverse.

BK: What is the difference between management and leadership? What do you consider yourself?

LB: Management is about the successful mechanics of managing effectively, and leadership is more about influencing masses and gaining their hearts and minds, so that they follow you as a role model in every step of the way even when you are not there because they respect you and they admire you. I consider myself a leader.

BK: What kind of performance management system do you use or recommend and why?

LB: At my organization, we use Management by Objectives. It is a great system to use because the manager and the employee know the expectations or goals in advance.

BK: What strategies do you recommend for maximizing productivity levels in the workforce?

LB: Keeping motivation high, keeping everybody on the same page through regular meetings, assessing performance through applicable measures, and giving feedback if there are any issues. These are some of the ways.

BK: Provide some examples of how you empower your employees.

LB: Letting them know about what they did great, treating them kindly and respectfully, and showing genuine concern for their problems.

BK: How do you reward your employees? Should rewards be based on merit?

LB: I am not in a position to reward anybody through raises just yet. I just give them positive feedback and provide guidance when I need an improvement or a change in things.

BK: What skills do new employees lack when they first enter the workforce? What recommendations do you have?

LB: Experience, speed, understanding individuals at work, learning how they operate and what the best way is to work with others. Careful observation, asking questions, taking good notes, practicing the steps involved, etc. A lot of these recommendations vary depending on the task.

BK: How can a leader influence and mold the culture of an organization?

LB: The leader needs to determine what aspects of the culture need reform and what aspects are assets to the institution and need to be maintained; and then come up with strategies that allow him/her to reform new strategies and maintain the well-functioning aspects.

BK: Can organizational politics help an organization?

LB: Yes. Understanding organizational politics can help a leader make more effective decisions.

BK: How important is teamwork in your profession?

LB: Very important. Each person contributes to a different step of the process and we all need to keep each other informed about our own portion throughout the whole process.

BK: Do you think your education has complemented your work experience or has your work experience complemented your education?

LB: I think my education has complemented my work experiences. I am not sure if it has a direct impact, but I do make use of different strategies that I acquired during my education.

BK: What motivates you to be successful?

LB: As I come across new challenges, I feel insufficient and I want to do better. I feel a need to improve myself and push myself further.

BK: If you could go back to college, what would you have majored in?

LB: I would have studied Strategic Management.

BK: Describe a typical day at work for you.

LB: I come to work at 7:30am and take care of my tasks and my to-do-list. My job involves a lot of interaction. I am communicating with people all day long. I focus on problem solving and I am task-oriented, so I feel very accomplished as I keep finishing off the tasks I need to complete. On most days, I don't even understand how the day goes by. I typically continue working and responding to emails when I go home.

BK: Where do you see yourself in 10 years?

LB: I hope to be a Dean or a CEO.

BK: What is your span of control?

LB: I have four people who report to me.

Notes

Karen Lewis is a Baby Boomer and has twelve years of management experience in Higher Education.

BK: Should leaders be more task or relationship oriented?

KL: Relationship-oriented. Leaders are skilled in relationship. Managers are more skilled with tasks.

BK: Based on your observations, is there still a glass ceiling in the workforce?

KL: Yes! We've made great strides over the years, but "the good 'ol boys" club is alive and well....and that club is usually white men. As a minority woman, I feel it from multiple angles.

BK: Based on your experiences, what is the best way to manage the different generations in the workforce?

KL: First, one must understand the differences between the generations – the values, the outlook on the world, the strengths and weaknesses of the different skill sets by generation. Secondly, the culture of an organization can impact this generational difference either positively or negatively. And finally, good executive leaders figure out ways to lead the managers who will be managing diverse groups.

BK: What generation are you from? What generation/category do the majority of your employees fall under?

KL: I am a Baby Boomer. In my last executive role, most employees were of the same generation. The greatest challenge I recall was with the Gen Y brats (oops, did I say that out loud?) This group, in my opinion, lacked the work ethic of my generation. They also felt entitled to special treatment, felt they deserved CEO positions simply because of who they were, not by what they'd accomplished. They seemed unskilled at problem solving, wanting quick answers without working it out.

BK: As a manager, how do you enhance motivation levels? Please provide some examples/stories.

KL: I think when you understand an employee's dreams – be it in the area of personal development or professional growth – and you acknowledge this, support it, talk about it, whatever…individuals are motivated in their current roles. People want to be contributors at work; they want to do good work. Most employees are not in their dream jobs. But if we as managers support their larger dreams, we are more likely to get the best version of them, now.

BK: What skills/traits do leaders need? How can a person develop his or her leadership skills?

KL: Leaders need a clear vision of where they're going. Leaders need to have the ability to enroll others in their vision. Leadership can be developed. I think leadership is a lifestyle, not a destination. The best training for leadership is to learn how to be a great follower. Following good leaders is the best training.

BK: Who is a leader that you admire and why? How has this person influenced your leadership style?

KL: Barack Obama. Anyone willing to risk his or her life for the greater good of a nation, of a planet, is worthy of my respect. He takes on his role as if he were the parent of a nation. He's able to assume a responsibility that very few of us could ever take on. We all possess his attributes. Any of us could be the President. We're just not willing to give our life in such a great way. He exudes sincerity, and is committed to serving ALL people, while keeping his ego in check. While this is a hard thing for me personally to embrace, it is something that has influenced my attempts to lead.

BK: Based on your experiences, how has the workforce changed over the years?

KL: I think many of us view "the workforce" from a narrow perspective. We get stuck in a paradigm of our own experience and are clueless about the many ways other organizations function. The workforce is comprised of PEOPLE.

BK: What is the difference between management and leadership? What do you consider yourself?

KL: Big difference. Managers focus on processes and systems; while leaders focus on people and vision. I consider myself to be both, but recognize the opportunity for growth in both areas.

BK: What kind of performance management system do you use or recommend and why?

KL: This concept is such a joke in most organizations I've worked in. I have too much emotional charge on the topic to even discuss today.

BK: What strategies do you recommend for maximizing productivity levels in the workforce?

KL: As I mentioned, I think when you understand an employee's dreams – be it in the area of professional growth or personal development – and you acknowledge this, support it, talk about it, whatever…individuals are motivated in their current roles.

BK: Provide some examples of how you empower your employees.

KL: By delegating responsibility, by truly being open to new ideas, by trusting them in their jobs (not micromanaging), by communicating clear expectations, by appreciating their personal life – approving time off, flexible scheduling, etc.

BK: How do you reward your employees? Should rewards be based on merit?

KL: Approving time off, awards with public and private acknowledgement, offering increased responsibility and/or opportunity. Some rewards are (and should be) merit based. For example, increases in salary may be based on measurable performance and metric achievement.

BK: What skills do new employees lack when they first enter the workforce? What recommendations do you have?

KL: I think the most common skill lacking in new employees is being able to relax, observe, and take notes, before trying to impose their expectations on long term employees who have not yet built trust and/or respect for the new employees.

BK: How can a leader influence and mold the culture of an organization?

KL: Good ol' leading by example comes to mind first. Also, I think good leaders have to recognize the current culture in order to influence and mold a new culture. A mistake leaders make is thinking they need to DO something to BE leaders, and sometimes what they need to do is to lay low and be the undercurrent, rather than the tidal wave.

BK: Can organizational politics help an organization?

KL: Of course. Good and evil live in all areas of our lives both professionally and personally. Politics is nothing but relationships and influence. Using power for good over evil is always an option.

BK: How important is teamwork in your profession?

KL: It's EVERYTHING. Departmental silos are an illusion.

BK: Do you think your education has complemented your work experience or has your work experience complemented your education?

KL: Absolutely! BA in Broadcasting + Graduate work in Career Development = excellent foundation for current role in current industry.

BK: What motivates you to be successful?

KL: A deep appreciation for life and the short amount of time we have on the planet in which to make a positive difference. Another motivator is love of God and an obedience to have a purpose filled life…serving His purpose. Yes, I said it!!!

BK: If you could go back to college, what would you have majored in?

KL: Very happy with my chosen majors.

BK: Where do you see yourself in 10 years?

KL: I'm not sure where I see myself in 10 years, as my priorities in life have shifted from a focus in the area of professional advancement to a more balanced, truly self-expressive family oriented life. Climbing the corporate ladder became an illusion, and in some cases, a nightmare.....a chasing rainbows experience. Recent events have put a bad taste in my mouth regarding being a pawn in a chess game that is not aligned with my greater goals in life, which have nothing to do with positions, titles, etc. I'm not yet ready to retire, but I am re-evaluating my goals. I find that my 10-year plan, which looked very clear a year ago, in now being reinvented.

BK: What is your span of control?

KL: I managed over 50 employees.

Notes

Michael Sabado is a Millennial and has eight years of experience in Healthcare Administration.

BK: Should leaders be more task or relationship oriented?

MS: Leaders should be more relationship oriented while managers should be more task oriented.

BK: Based on your observations, is there still a glass ceiling in the workforce?

MS: I have a very neutral response to this question. I have seen many female managers obtain top leadership positions in my organization. There are many more males in high ranking positions but it's not apparent to me that it's because of the lack of opportunity.

BK: Based on your experiences, what is the best way to manage the different generations in the workforce?

MS: Older generations like Baby Boomers seem to be more comfortable with a hierarchy based organization and younger generations do better in a flatter management structure. Older generations seem to be okay with being told what to do and younger generations like to be a part of developing the process.

BK: What generation are you from? What generation/category do the majority of your employees fall under? Has this caused any problems?

MS: Generation Y. Most of the employees in my area are Baby Boomers. This has caused low or slow adoption rates of newer technology. Since many technology leaders are less interested in proactively adopting newer technology, the organization is usually left making reactive decisions. Furthermore, implementing change or adopting new ideas is usually viewed as disruptive to older employees and exciting to younger employees.

BK: As a manager, how do you enhance motivation levels? Please provide some examples/stories.

MS: The best way I've found to enhance motivation is by breaking relationship barriers and setting baseline competencies so that more effective teams are formed. When a team is more effective, the individual employees tend to be more motivated. The most recent example I have is when I was recently promoted to a department with an older peer group. Enhancing motivation was as simple as teaching my peers new skills and offering my assistance as much as possible. My energy spread across the department resulting in increased collaboration among all members of the team.

BK: What skills/traits do leaders need? How can a person develop his or her leadership skills?

MS: Leaders should be technically competent over the organization that they are leading as well as being educated in management theory. Effective leaders empower their employees as stewards of the work over straight delegation. A person needs both experience and the willingness to research/learn new management theory at all times to keep them from stagnating.

BK: Who is a leader that you admire and why? How has this person influenced your leadership style?

MS: A leader that I admire is the vice president of technology for my organization. She has a strong technical competency but her relationship building capabilities make her an admirable leader. When working in task groups with her, she respects the knowledge that everyone brings to the table and empowers people to work at their maximum potential. She has taught me to respect the people that I work with as functionally adequate so that I can focus on their potential and not on their shortcomings.

BK: Based on your experiences, how has the workforce changed over the years?

MS: The newer workforce seems less formal and less disciplined. Younger workers look to be respected as an individual and their special needs to be taken into consideration. They are more focused on being creative in the workplace than showing up on time. The younger workforce is willing to change and learn new things. They bring tremendous value to departments with older workers and help with change initiatives requiring teaching new skills and processes.

BK: What is the difference between management and leadership? What do you consider yourself?

MS: Management is making sure that specific tasks are accomplished to meet a certain metric. This includes overseeing the performance of frontline staff and day-to-day activities. Leadership is focused on empowering and supporting front line managers. Leadership is also responsible for setting the overall objectives and steering the organization in a purpose based objective. I consider myself a leader because I influence policy and empower other managers to perform to their full potential by way of technology.

BK: What kind of performance management system do you use or recommend and why?

MS: Salesforce has a product called Work.com that a colleague of mine shared with me. The software is based on principles that my organization is trying to set. For instance, it offers real-time coaching of employees and a more motivational approach to performance recognition. The application is very socially interactive so younger employees will feel more at home with the social networking influenced experience.

BK: What strategies do you recommend for maximizing productivity levels in the workforce?

MS: The best strategy that I have found for maximizing productivity is by watching what the most productive employees are doing. Then I focus on the most unproductive employees. By recognizing the gaps and barriers of unproductive employees, I can better influence what was learned from the more productive employees. My observation has been that lower producing employees also have the lowest competency in the work that they are involved in. Increasing their competency with cross training or third party training usually helps.

BK: Provide some examples of how you empower your employees.

MS: One way that I empower employees is by stepping back and asking for their input often and by giving them an opportunity to teach me their processes. I serve only as a supportive influence and help guide them as necessary. An example is a strategy that I use quite often. I have projects that involve many technicians. I ask the technicians to tell me how they would solve the problem given all of the artifacts of the situation. I also tell them that I will support their process as long as it's logical and non-disruptive. They usually come back with more effective solutions than I would be able to come up with by myself.

BK: How do you reward your employees? Should rewards be based on merit?

MS: I recognize employee accomplishments first on a team level. If a team member goes above and beyond I will reward that individual in front of the team after the team recognition. Rewards should absolutely be based on merit because the strongest performers will set the pace for the rest of the team.

BK: What skills do new employees lack when they first enter the workforce? What recommendations do you have?

MS: Younger employees tend to be highly energetic around creative work but lose that energy around the monotonous daily activities. For example, younger employees are less inclined to fill out the paperwork that must be done but will focus more on creative ways that the paperwork will be automated. We have a computer refresh project that has to be accomplished every year. The instructions are simple—replace the current aging computers with a newer computer. The younger technicians are so focused on developing tools to make the job easier that they are less concerned on the work actually getting done. The recommendation I have is to set the target and deadline expectations up front but in small increments.

BK: How can a leader influence and mold the culture of an organization?

MS: A leader can influence the culture of an organization by working with other leaders to develop the culture. Getting buy-in from every level of the organization is the key and including frontline staff will increase the likeliness of the culture's long term effectiveness. Having a principle centered mission statement of the culture change will also contribute to its effectiveness.

BK: Can organizational politics help an organization?

MS: Organizational politics can be a benefit only if the message is aligned to the mission.

BK: How important is teamwork in your profession?

MS: Teamwork is the most essential component of my profession. I work in a very technical department and no one person knows the solution to every problem. Most of the solutions that we generate are a collaborative effort.

BK: Do you think your education has complemented your work experience or has your work experience complemented your education?

MS: My early education was very technical and that allowed me to get an entry level job to start building my work experience. Later on in my career, my work experience provided context for my education.

BK: What motivates you to be successful?

MS: I am a life-long learner so an opportunity to learn new things in my current position keeps me motivated. I really enjoy building new relationships and learning from other people.

BK: If you could go back to college, what would you have majored in?

MS: I would have majored in Computer Science. I know that I had the discipline right out of college to complete that degree. I think I would have had more to offer to my organization and my personal interests by having an engineering degree.

BK: Describe a typical day at work for you.

MS: I usually start off the day reviewing the tasks that I have to accomplish for the day and what is scheduled on my calendar. Then I write those items in a book listed by priority and urgency. A lot of the morning consists of going through emails and getting status updates on projects. I meet with my team to see if there is anything that I can help them with. I travel to face-to-face meetings or I meet via web conferencing.

BK: Where do you see yourself in 10 years?

MS: In 10 years, I see myself at a senior management/executive level. I really want to stay in Information Technology but I would not be opposed to contributing to hospital administration.

BK: What is your span of control?

MS: I have virtual oversight of 30+ employees including managers and field technicians. I lead a group of three consultants and one project manager under the IT Director. I am a point of escalation and approval for several technology domains. I have direct influence for technology related matters for two medical centers and eight clinics. My peer group consists of senior leaders, service directors, and managers.

Notes

Joe Tyler is from Generation X and has twelve years of management experience in Healthcare Administration.

BK: Should leaders be more task or relationship oriented?

JT: In this day and time, I'm finding that leaders should be more relationship oriented. Employees like to feel comfortable with the leader they report to and I believe an effort can be made towards this if you build a solid working relationship with your team. It can simply be done by taking an employee to lunch for their 1:1 sessions.

BK: Based on your observations, is there still a glass ceiling in the workforce?

JT: I would agree with this from a half and half perspective. Women have come a long way in organizations today. There are several women who are top level executives in organizations today. For instance, if you take a look at the Health Plan Insurance industry, you will find several women at the top. Prior to its Interim President/CEO, WellPoint, Inc. recently had a woman as the President/CEO/Chairman of the Board (Angela Braly). She sat in the seat for five years. That's a pretty long time for a CEO at a large organization such as WellPoint, Inc. Furthermore, WellPoint, Inc. still continues to move forward with four women on the Executive Leadership Team (ELT). There was a time when the ELT only had men. As for minorities, this is still an issue for several organizations. WellPoint did have a few minorities on the ELT but they are all gone at this point. It seems most organizations have a

Diversity Officer or some type of Diversity arm in the organization but it never seems to address the lack of Diversity on the ELT. This is one area that needs to improve tremendously.

BK: Based on your experiences, what is the best way to manage the different generations in the workforce?

JT: I believe a leader must hold 1:1 sessions consistently with the different generations as an effort to manage them. It would allow the leader/manager to learn the differences in the generations (likes/dislikes) and in turn allow the leader to manage accordingly.

BK: What generation are you from? What generation/category do the majority of your employees fall under? Has this caused any problems?

JT: I'm from Generation X. I've always managed employees from Generation X. I've had issues with this generation because it seems to me that if a leader is from this generation and then has to manage staff from this generation, it may cause issues. I've had an issue with an employee trying to undermine me or not follow my lead on directions that were clearly stated. Basically, the employee wanted to do things the way she wanted them done. The end result of the particular issue ended up in disciplinary action for the employee.

BK: As a manager, how do you enhance motivation levels? Please provide some examples/stories.

JT: I utilize R&Rs. Rewards and Recognition is the key to motivating staff. For instance, if satisfaction surveys from customers/clients show consistent improvement over time, I award my staff with gift cards or a day to leave early with no dock in pay.

BK: What skills/traits do leaders need? How can a person develop his or her leadership skills?

JT: Leaders should lead more and manage less, be able to articulate a clear vision and inspire others, keep things simple, be less formal, and see change as an opportunity. A good start for an individual to get the skills he/she needs to become a top notch leader is mentorship. If you know of anyone in your organization who is an Executive Leader and one that inspires you, reach out to him/her to see if they have the time to become your mentor.

BK: Who is a leader that you admire and why? How has this person influenced your leadership style?

JT: Jack Welch is a leader that I've come to love and admire. Mr. Welch managed GE for a very long time and it was a successful organization that consistently ran smoothly. After learning more about Jack Welch's leadership style, I adopted some of his business practices.

BK: Based on your experiences, how has the workforce changed over the years?

JT: The workforce has changed tremendously over the years. I can remember a time when you could go into an organization and apply for a job, be interviewed, and hired on the spot. Today it's not like that. Most organizations will hold a phone screening with you and may do this a couple of times before they have you come in for an in person interview. They also tend to want you to fill everything out online. The process seemed to move much faster when you would go in to fill out an application. Now the process could take weeks before you actually receive an interview.

BK: What is the difference between management and leadership? What do you consider yourself?

JT: Management simply means you manage and leadership refers to leading. When I think of management I think of a manager who watches their employees closely; who is somewhat of a micro-manager. A leader will lead a team/group and does not micromanage. A real leader develops staff members for the next level. I'm a firm believer of getting the best out of an employee who is a happy employee. I see myself as a leader.

BK: What kind of performance management system do you use or recommend and why?

JT: I prefer the quarterly performance management system. As for performance, I believe it's important for an employee to know where he or she stands at all times. Most people will do a yearly evaluation. If quarterly seems to be a bit much, then at least do a Mid-Year Performance Review with the employee. It's important for employees to know how they are doing at all times.

BK: What strategies do you recommend for maximizing productivity levels in the workforce?

JT: Holding consistent 1:1 sessions with employees and discussing how to help an employee reach his/her potential. Also, creating teams and competitions in a department helps to maximize productivity levels.

BK: Provide some examples of how you empower your employees.

JT: I always share my perspective on issues when employees ask at the end of the day. I've allowed employees to make decisions and take ownership. I always let them know that it is his/her decision but I'd like him/her to be accountable for the decision.

BK: How do you reward your employees? Should rewards be based on merit?

JT: I award employees by Impact or Values in Action Awards. It does not have to be based on merit. It can simply be something specific that he or she did for a client, the company, or another team member.

BK: What skills do new employees lack when they first enter the workforce? What recommendations do you have?

JT: What I've noticed is that most employees lack communication skills. After a comprehensive training from Human Resources, I'd recommend pairing up new employees with the older employees to help them learn the ropes.

BK: How can a leader influence and mold the culture of an organization?

JT: By always staying energized and communicating a clear vision for the organization.

BK: Can organizational politics help an organization?

JT: No. I always say keep the politics out of the work environment. It causes friction among a team and it is a way to divide an organization.

BK: How important is teamwork in your profession?

JT: My work really does not require a team as I now have a position where I'm an individual contributor. I'm my own team and that actually is just as important as a team of two or more.

BK: Do you think your education has complemented your work experience or has your work experience complemented your education?

JT: Well for me, I would have to say that my education complemented my work experience. For a very long time, I worked while I pursued my education.

BK: What motivates you to be successful?

JT: I was raised on a tobacco farm where my parents had hired help and also used their children to work as well. It was very hard field work and it encouraged me to always seek higher education so that I wouldn't have to work that hard.

BK: If you could go back to college, what would you have majored in?

JT: I would have majored in Education.

BK: Describe a typical day at work for you.

JT: My typical day includes pulling down contractual negotiations from a queue that consists of incomplete medical coding. I pull about 10 to 12 contractual negotiations down per day and provide a comprehensive analysis and provide coding recommendations to the Contract Director.

BK: Where do you see yourself in 10 years?

JT: I hope to be an Executive Leader at a Community College. I'm currently pursuing a doctoral degree in Education with an emphasis in Community College Leadership.

BK: What is your span of control?

JT: Currently, I don't manage staff. I'm an individual contributor but I've managed between one to eight people at a time in my past roles.

Notes

Karen Hesse is a Baby Boomer and has seven years of management experience in Higher Education.

BK: Should leaders be more task or relationship oriented?

KH: I don't think leaders can ignore either. They need to be able to focus on the tasks that need to be accomplished while developing relationships with their team members. If a leader has a good relationship with her/his team, that leader may be able to elicit the best from each team member. As an educator, I think relationships are very important. I felt I could help more students if I built relationships with the students. They would see me as someone they could ask for assistance. I think that was a successful approach because students sought me out for assistance.

BK: Based on your observations, is there still a glass ceiling in the workforce?

KH: Yes. In my field, private sector education, women were often the campus leaders and one rare exception was a regional manager. However, men are found at the highest echelons of management, although it is primarily women who are found in the upper ranks of the curriculum team. I don't recall seeing many men of color in the higher ranks nor openly gay or lesbian people. It really seemed like it was an old boy network in that certain people could rise through the ranks to the top levels if they knew the higher level managers in some way. When the company was purchased by a larger company, rising through the ranks stopped as the new corporation brought in their own people to manage my original company. Now the only people rising in rank are those who know people in the larger company. In other organizations, it may be different. I think it depends on the culture of the organization. Right now, for example, I am involved with the Private Industry Council as a client. As far as I can see, it is extremely diverse. The new supervisor is a young woman of Asian descent. The employees are young and old and of all ethnicities. They all seem to like and respect their supervisor.

BK: Based on your experiences, what is the best way to manage the different generations in the workforce?

KH: I treated all my employees as I would want to be treated. I think that is the only way to manage a diverse workforce. Even though someone may be of a certain generation or ethnic background, if you treat them like capable individuals, I believe they will respond to that. When I interviewed them, I learned their personalities (to an extent), abilities, and interests. Some people wanted more interaction and some less. I didn't want to be like my own supervisor who micromanaged. I made sure each person knew what they needed to do and that they had the tools to do their jobs. I also tried to be available to them so they could debrief if needed.

BK: What generation are you from? What generation/category do the majority of your employees fall under? Has this caused any problems?

KH: I'm a Baby Boomer. Most of my staff were younger, both Gen X and Gen Y. I didn't see any generational problems, but of course there may have been but not brought up to me. My employees were adjuncts who came in to teach their class and left to go to their next assignment of the day. It is possible if we had more contact, there might have been more conflict, but looking back on interactions, I believe we all treated one another respectfully and professionally. I think everyone had the same notion of what professionalism was. There was one incident in which a new instructor wore inappropriate clothing for our workplace. The students who complained were all her generation, so I'm not sure if that was a generational thing. I reminded her of the dress code and she complied.

BK: As a manager, how do you enhance motivation levels? Please provide some examples/stories.

KH: I try to recognize accomplishments. When we earned Department of the Quarter, I made sure everyone knew it was not just me but everyone who earned that award. If students really liked an instructor, I made sure the instructor knew and even let that instructor read the feedback if written. I nominated my staff every quarter for awards but no one was ever chosen.

BK: What skills/traits do leaders need? How can a person develop his or her leadership skills?

KH: That is a good question. I think we often learn to lead or manage through trial and error. Having said that, I think leaders need lots of patience because their employees will not always understand what they need to do or know how to do it. Leaders have to be willing to train and provide feedback even when the employee doesn't want to listen. Leaders also need to listen. I recall a time when I was accused of being negative because as a counselor I pointed out a behavior sequence I had seen among our residents. The girls seemed to never fit in at their first residence; they acted out. I pointed out that our new resident was displaying the same pattern and suggested we should move her to another house – which was ultimately what happened and she was very happy there. At the time however, everyone, including my supervisor, thought I was wrong and they ignored my suggestion until they had no other choice but to move the girl.

BK: Who is a leader that you admire and why? How has this person influenced your leadership style?

KH: I don't know of anyone in particular. There was a former dean who was always cheerful and pleasant. She had a lot of energy. Her demeanor, though, was why people wanted to work for her.

BK: Based on your experiences, how has the workforce changed over the years?

KH: It's hard for me to say. I spent 10 years working in retail and social services, and then another 10 years in a blue collar occupation before working in education. Those experiences colored my view of the workforce. However, I can say my earlier experiences were of female workers with male supervisors. In fact, I remember a scandal at a store I worked in where a male department head was paid more because he was male. His female counterpart earned substantially less. She was told that he was expected to support a family and she wasn't; of course, he was a single person living with his parents and she had children to support. That still exists to an extent. Today, it still seems to be a "female ghetto" in certain fields like child care or education, and again, the few men in the field move up rapidly. I believe employers today, for the most part, are seeing that people of all types can contribute. As an unemployed person, I see some discrimination based on age. Older workers are not being hired, even those only in their early forties. The workforce is becoming younger as a result. Also, in some fields it is nearly impossible to get a position without a terminal degree. People need to be well educated in today's economy. Another thing I see happening is the narrow definition of how some occupations are defined. A person must have very specific education and/or experience. It is more difficult to parlay one's skills into a new occupation. This is perhaps because we have more workers that work in the United States, and probably globally as well.

BK: What is the difference between management and leadership? What do you consider yourself?

KH: Well, I've read the literature. Managers have employees, leaders have followers. I think a successful manager will have leadership qualities and be able to persuade and inspire people to do their best, meet goals or rise to the challenge. Conversely, leaders still need to manage. I prefer to think of it as knowing what needs to be done and selecting a way to get the job done. Each employee (or follower) is individual and will respond differently. You need to treat each person respectfully and in a way that enables them to reach their potential.

BK: What kind of performance management system do you use or recommend and why?

KH: I prefer Management by Objectives.

BK: What strategies do you recommend for maximizing productivity levels in the workforce?

KH: I think this gets to an issue of integrity. Is maximizing productivity ethical? I have quandaries about this. Increased productivity seems to be fewer people doing more work and working longer hours to do that work. Maybe we need to be less productive and put more people to work. Now I'm not in favor of deliberate sabotage as I saw in the printing trade. When guys needed overtime, they "blew up" the presses repeatedly all night long. An eight hour shift easily turned into twelve hours. That is wrong, too. I think people should do the job they are paid to do and the employer should respect his/her workers. Looking back, I think a workplace can be more productive if employees feel valued. I don't mean the awards that always go to the same people that my last employer gave out quarterly. Recognition is nice but employees know they are valued when they are paid and treated fairly.

BK: Provide some examples of how you empower your employees.

KH: This question reminds me of two situations: one where a given student felt I gave too much support to the teacher and the other one is where the teacher felt I was siding too much with the students. I guess I trusted my teachers. I let them teach how they wanted to teach, using whatever tools they preferred. One man created elaborate portfolios with his students which took a lot of time, but if they learned what they were supposed to, then it doesn't matter how the class is taught. Another instructor used debates and films a lot. It's not my style, but if you hire experts in their fields, you have to trust them to do the right thing and do it well. When I had to oversee student workers, I observed what they did and suggested changes in private, when they were needed. I also recognized their achievements. Many times they had ideas I would never have thought of trying.

BK: How do you reward your employees? Should rewards be based on merit?

KH: The only way I could reward employees was through recognition or offering them more work. I had no control over pay or anything else. I regularly submitted names to the campus recognition committee. I'd also tell them that they had done well, which was about all I could do. We had student surveys which students generally use to complain about instructors. I told students if they liked someone, they should say so. That way I would know who to hire again.

BK: What skills do new employees lack when they first enter the workforce? What recommendations do you have?

KH: They lack confidence and knowledge of the company's culture and procedures. Procedures can be taught. Confidence comes with success and support. New teachers often had no idea how to manage a class so I developed a bank of materials for them as well as a list of common procedures and duties. I tried to support the teachers as much as possible and tried to guide them. Of course, sometimes new staff resented that. I had to learn how to be very tactful. One instructor spoke to the ceiling in class every day and took offense when I suggested alternatives.

BK: How can a leader influence and mold the culture of an organization?

KH: Unless the culture is deeply engrained, I think leaders shape the culture simply by example. If a leader is

174

respectful, then the organization responds. I spoke to an employee at a local company who was very enthusiastic about the owner. He made the effort to learn everyone's names, promoted from within and treated everyone respectfully. The woman with whom I spoke marveled over the fact that he knew her name and gave her the opportunity to move up.

BK: Can organizational politics help an organization?

KH: I don't think so. I think people become enmeshed in petty squabbles over territory or perks. It can interfere with the job and make other people uncomfortable. However, I probably benefited from them because a lot of people spoke up on my behalf when I was being considered for the position as Director of General Education.

BK: How important is teamwork in your profession?

KH: It depends on the position. As a teacher or professor, you're alone in the classroom and pretty much do everything on your own. The teacher can choose how to teach the curriculum so it is pretty autonomous. As a department, teamwork is everything. One person can't accomplish everything. The tasks need to be shared and people have to work together. If I had a student at risk, I worked with other directors and instructors to reach out and help the student.

BK: Do you think your education has complemented your work experience or has your work experience complemented your education?

KH: I think it goes both ways. I couldn't have had the position I held without the education I had. However, I wouldn't be the person I am without the experiences I've had.

BK: What motivates you to be successful?

KH: Pride and a desire to be of use. Pride because I try to do my best and I would feel bad if I didn't give it my best effort. Also, a desire to be of use because I want to help people succeed. I think anyone in education is in the field because of the students. We want to see our students graduate and succeed.

BK: If you could go back to college, what would you have majored in?

KH: I would love to have a doctoral degree in education or psychology. I'd like to contribute to the advances in education and cognition so that many more people could achieve their potential. However, sometimes I think sociology, economics and political science would help me understand the changes taking place in today's society.

At any rate, a doctoral degree would enable me to stay in higher education as a teacher. Because I don't have one, I am seeking other employment now. I have thought about pursuing the degree, but the cost is too much; it just doesn't make sense to go into debt to work only part time as an adjunct, especially at my age.

BK: Describe a typical day at work for you.

KH: That is so long ago now. And it changed from the beginning to the end. In the beginning, a typical day would be observing classes, answering the phone calls, checking emails, and calling teachers. I rescheduled students, evaluated transcripts, and sometimes printed out documents for students. At the end, I spent the day in the library or learning lab. I answered questions, fixed the copier numerous times, and tutored several students daily.

On Fridays, I called all the at-risk online students asking them to see me or a tutor for help and offered assistance over the phone. Fridays were eight hours of phone calls.

BK: Where do you see yourself in 10 years?

KH: I'm not feeling optimistic. I hope that I can afford to retire in 10 years, but I expect one of two things. I will either still be unemployed as it becomes more difficult to be hired the longer one is out of work, or I will be underemployed. There are hundreds of applicants for every position I apply for and it is difficult to compete successfully against younger applicants. They have fewer health problems and lower expectations. It seems employers prefer those qualities to experience. However, I am seeking retraining through the Workforce Investment Act and may be gainfully employed after earning a certificate in another profession.

BK: What is your span of control?

KH: I never managed more than a handful of people at a time. I was constantly hiring to replace the people who couldn't survive on occasional work as an adjunct instructor. If the students are included into the mix, I managed a hundred or so at a given time.

Notes

Phyllis Duryee is a Baby Boomer who has thirty years of management experience in Higher Education.

BK: Should leaders be more task or relationship oriented?

PD: In my view, leaders need to be relationship oriented. If they are too task oriented, they lose sight of their management goals, which have to be successful through people and teams, not through the tasks that they do.

BK: Based on your observations, is there still a glass ceiling in the workforce?

PD: Most definitely. Even in higher education where you would think women and minorities would have made the most progress, you find cracks in the ceiling, but not much break through.

BK: Based on your experiences, what is the best way to manage the different generations in the workforce?

PD: Leaders need to learn more about the upcoming generations, what motivates them, and what kind of work environment they desire. Too many older leaders think that upcoming generations should want the same kind of work style that they had.

BK: What generation are you from? What generation/category do the majority of your employees fall under?

PD: I am from the Boomer generation and I manage a diverse group of faculty members.

BK: Has this caused any problems?

PD: I don't think it has caused many problems.

BK: Please elaborate as much as possible.

PD: I try to stay as connected as possible with young people and get an understanding of the problems they face today.

BK: Give examples.

PD: I try to stay updated with new technology, with cheaper ways of doing things. For example, using an eTextbook has made it cheaper for my students.

BK: As a manager, how do you enhance motivation levels? Please provide some examples/stories.

PD: I try to lead by example. I can't expect people to work hard if I don't. I also try to do the same in my classes. If my work is not exemplary, I can't expect my students to do outstanding work either.

BK: What skills/traits do leaders need? How can a person develop his or her leadership skills?

PD: It is difficult for me to say what skills leaders need. In my opinion, leaders are born with many of those traits naturally. Mentoring for someone who has those traits certainly helps. However, the desire and motivation to lead must be inherent within a person.

BK: Who is a leader that you admire and why? How has this person influenced your leadership style?

PD: There are probably many people I can name, but I would have to say that the person who has influenced my leadership style the most is my husband. He is a natural leader, but he is quiet about it. He started by being a professional in the Boy Scouts of America. Perhaps that is where he honed his skills. Then his leadership in government positions has enhanced those skills. I am amazed at the number of people who say that he changed their lives in a substantial way.

BK: Based on your experiences, how has the workforce changed over the years?

PD: It has become easier for women and minorities. That is not to say that women and minorities are where they should be in our society, but considering what women and minorities of my age went through, I think that is where most of the great strides have been made.

BK: What is the difference between management and leadership? What do you consider yourself?

PD: Managers are all about tasks. Leaders are all about where the organization is headed in the future.

BK: What kind of performance management system do you use or recommend and why?

PD: One that provides incentive to everyone who contributes to an organization's success, but also gives a little extra to those folks who do an outstanding job in a given year.

BK: What strategies do you recommend for maximizing productivity levels in the workforce?

PD: Providing the resources needed to do the job.

BK: Provide some examples of how you empower your employees.

PD: Letting them know often how much they are appreciated and thanking them for a good job when it is deserved.

BK: How do you reward your employees? Should rewards be based on merit?

PD: In my position I don't have much opportunity to make this decision, but in determining awards to adjunct faculty, the criteria have already been set. It is a matter of determining who meets the criteria.

BK: What skills do new employees lack when they first enter the workforce? What recommendations do you have?

PD: Everyone needs on-the-job training that is sufficient to make them successful in the jobs they are expected to do.

BK: How can a leader influence and mold the culture of an organization?

PD: The leader, along with others in the organization, should have a mission and some general goals to achieve. When everyone is on the same page, they can truly accomplish great things.

BK: Can organizational politics help an organization?

PD: I suppose it can, but I've seen nearly every kind of structure for an organization and they all have their problems.

BK: How important is teamwork in your profession?

PD: Very important. I couldn't work without a team of professionals around me.

BK: Do you think your education has complemented your work experience or has your work experience complemented your education?

PD: I think that both have occurred at different times in my life. In general though, work opportunities have allowed me to use my education.

BK: What motivates you to be successful?

PD: An innate desire to do well.

BK: If you could go back to college, what would you have majored in?

PD: I would have gotten a PhD in psycho-linguistics.

BK: Describe a typical day at work for you.

PD: Answer emails first and then go to planned meetings. I then spend much of my day teaching, answering student questions, and doing committee work.

BK: Where do you see yourself in 10 years?

PD: Retired!

BK: What is your span of control?

PD: About 45 faculty members who teach Global Issues.

Notes

Lisa Jensen Cook is a Baby Boomer and has over ten years of management experience in Higher Education.

BK: Should leaders be more task or relationship oriented?

LC: I think that leaders have to be both relationship and task oriented. They need to be task oriented in order to get assigned work completed in a timely manner because their own job performance is based to some degree on the performance of their subordinates. But they also need to be relationship oriented because they are dealing with human beings who both want and need to be reminded of the good work they are doing; this helps in building a working rapport with their supervisors.

BK: Based on your observations, is there still a glass ceiling in the workforce?

LC: There is definitely a glass ceiling as far as management in the workforce. I notice that there was a distinctly different pay rate between men and women performing the same job when I was the Dean of Education and had to hire some Program Directors. Why, one of the directors was hired by me but made more money than me and I was his supervisor! I was told that the reasoning behind this was the fact that he had a Master's degree; when I explained that I too had a Master's degree I was told that he had several more years of management experience than I did (which ended up not being true at all). In all reality, he had the degree that they needed to begin a new program on the campus and he refused to start for any less money, so they happily paid him about $22,000 more per year than what I was making.

BK: Based on your experiences, what is the best way to manage the different generations in the workforce?

LC: My experience shows that the best way to manage different generations in the same workforce is to specifically "buddy up" a younger member with an older one as a mentor team, explaining that over time, the two of them will learn new techniques and skills from each other. This usually works just fine with very few bumps in the road. However, my staff, no matter their generation, needs to know that I am approachable and will listen both to their concerns and their suggestions to improve our working environment.

BK: What generation are you from? What generation/category do the majority of your employees fall under? Has this caused any problems?

LC: I am a proud Baby Boomer, born right smack in the middle, in the year 1955. Most of my employees have been either Baby Boomers or Generation X's with a very few Generation Y's. This is because I work in the education environment and many of the younger people are still working on earning their own degrees from my school. One of the differences I have noticed is that Baby Boomers tend to have a much stronger work ethic that those in the "Generations". Perhaps it is because we were born in the lean years after WWII when jobs were still scarce and we had to fight to keep them. I have seen many Boomers come to work when they should be in bed because they are ill; they don't want to burden their co-workers with picking up the slack from them being gone for the day. However, Boomers don't stop to think that they are probably infecting many of their co-workers by being there and also that their productivity is sadly decreased due to their lack of feeling well. We should learn to take care of ourselves at home, even if that means calling in sick for the day. Boomers also seem to have a vested interest in customer service and satisfaction; this is perhaps because they don't plan on switching jobs in the future. The younger generations folks are just in the early stages of their career and they know that the odds are they will change jobs or careers at least three times during their working life; therefore, they don't seem quite so concerned with their performance.

BK: As a manager, how do you enhance motivation levels? Please provide some examples/stories.

LC: Over the years, I have had the opportunity to watch many managers and I have learned a lot. One of the most important and positive things I have learned is that it is so important to let your employee know when they have done a good job. Many times managers get so busy or are under so much pressure to perform from their supervisors, that they only notice when their employee has done something wrong. It doesn't take long for the employee to catch on that their manager only wants to speak to them when they have done something wrong; this leads to apprehension and indifferent attitudes from the employees. I think that each person deserves recognition for a job well done, so long as it is sincere and meaningful. I try to find some way every day to touch bases with each of my employees and I let them know when I have seen them go out of their way to extend customer service or assist a coworker or student. Even my more challenging employees deserve to be told when they are working on a previously discussed inadequacy and there is improvement. I don't think that managers realize how much their opinions matter to their staff. As an example, a Program Director has hanging on her bulletin board a little index card-sized thank you note from me for taking care of ordering the monthly office supplies for the entire faculty room. Not an unusual detail, except for the fact that I gave her that card back in 2006 when I was the Dean!

BK: What skills/traits do leaders need? How can a person develop his or her leadership skills?

LC: Skills and traits for a good leader have to include integrity, so your staff can be assured that you are treating them fairly and with respect; empathy, so that your staff knows that you have 'been there' before and have learned from your mistakes; honesty, so your staff knows that you are beyond reproach; enthusiasm for the job, which will motivate your employees to also become enthusiastic; willingness to grow and expand your horizons, the ability to think outside of the box; and loyalty, to your employees, your institution, and yourself. A person can develop leadership skills by attending the various available motivational seminars or company-sponsored leadership conferences. I know that I learn something new every time I attend one of these meetings.

BK: Who is a leader that you admire and why? How has this person influenced your leadership style?

LC: I admire Secretary of State, Hillary Clinton because she has been in some difficult situations and rather than run from them has chosen to stop, face the problem head-on, find the proper solution and then grow exponentially with each challenge she faces. She is someone who definitely thinks outside of the box; she encourages her staff, her daughter, and indeed the women of America to be the best they can be. And her campaign goal back in 2008 was to shatter the glass ceiling for women in the workforce and we came pretty close. Now she is still hard at work fighting for human rights (those of men, women, and children) both here in America and around the world.

BK: Based on your experiences, how has the workforce changed over the years?

LC: My working career has stretched from 1971 until now, 2012; for 41 years I have been paying into Social Security, while having a variety of jobs and I can say that there have been many changes. From the most obvious: my first hourly pay rate when I was a kid working as a waitress was $.90 per hour! People no longer seem to take pride in the work that they do now; they feel that they work their job in order to supply their needs and wants. So the actual loyalty I used to see from workers regarding their place of employment and their individual jobs seem to have lessened in importance. Especially during the past 9-10 years: people work to live; they no longer live to work. A career, no matter how insignificant used to be a source of pride; now folks seem almost embarrassed to reveal where they work, unless of course they are making a six-figure income in some executive position.

BK: What is the difference between management and leadership? What do you consider yourself?

LC: Management is concerned with the bottom line as far as finances are concerned. Everything about the job revolves around profit and gains (or losses). When management eliminates jobs due to the economic downturn, they say "It's not personal; it is just business." But we all know that it is very personal to the person whose job has been eliminated. In leadership, the primary concern is for the workers and their productivity. Leaders will assist their workers in performing the very best that they can. I can again use my campus as an example of the difference between management and leadership: the Executive Director is responsible for the "numbers"; whether it is the number of students, the number of excess inventory, the number of outstanding payments overdue, or the reduction of staff as it is necessary to reduce the amount of money being spent by the campus versus how much money the campus is making each month. The Dean of Education (Academic Affairs) is in charge of the leadership portion of the campus: leader for the students, including reducing fails or student withdrawals, and ensuring that the student is paying any outstanding debts. The Dean is also primarily responsible for leading the staff and faculty of the education department. This involves everything from monthly meetings with program directors all the way to counseling sessions for new or young faculty members to train them in how to keep the students engaged and coming to school on a daily basis. I consider myself to be a member of the leadership category because I am concerned with my students and staff and I let the people on the Campus Management Team (CMT) run the financial end.

BK: What kind of performance management system do you use or recommend and why?

LC: I recommend using a 360-degree feedback system because it is the fairest way to assess performance. On our campuses, employees were required to complete a yearly self-evaluation where they determined their areas of growth over the previous year. They also had to list the areas where they knew there could be improvements made and then they listed these improvements as their goals for the upcoming year. This self-evaluation was always completed before the yearly management reviews and annual wage increases. The manager would complete their own review of their employee's performance, including asking impartial staff members their official evaluation of that specific staff member. That evaluation would include such areas as: give an example of an area where you noticed this staff member had improved their performance this year. In this way the managers could gather information that perhaps they hadn't had a chance to observe and together with the employee's self-evaluation and their own formal observations could complete this yearly evaluation, "grading" the staff member's performance over the past twelve months. This evaluation package would then be passed through the ranks of management with the ultimate decision of the employee's pay increase being decided by the Executive Director and based on the percentage of available funds for increases.

BK: What strategies do you recommend for maximizing productivity levels in the workforce?

LC: Positive reinforcement that is sincerely delivered will go a long way in encouraging my staff and faculty to give 110% every day. I also think that salaries should be commensurate with an employee's experience and productiveness at work; they should not be based on a pay scale decided by some group of administrators who work in the ivory tower and have no idea what faculty and staff accomplish in their departments. I also think that monetary and recognition rewards should be employed in an effort to call attention to exemplary behavior and/or performance.

BK: Provide some examples of how you empower your employees.

LC: My strongest tool of empowerment is that I encourage my employees to teach to the classroom, not to the curriculum. As any educator knows, no two students learn in the same manner; therefore, no two classrooms can be successful with canned material delivered in the same manner every day. In other words, I give my staff academic freedom to deliver material in the way they see best fits their classroom of students with the codicil that all required material must be covered in some way so that students are successful on tests and other evaluations. I also empower my staff to make their own decisions on how to manage their classrooms, again with the reminder that the school rules must ultimately be followed.

BK: How do you reward your employees? Should rewards be based on merit?

LC: I reward my employees by treating them and their knowledge with respect. I allow them to take longer lunch periods or the opportunity to arrive late or leave early from school when it is not going to affect student learning outcomes. Rewards should be based on merit; however, in this current economy one does not usually have the opportunity to offer their employees monetary rewards. Therefore, allowing them freedom to make their own decisions (within reason of course) goes a long way toward showing your appreciation for a job well done.

BK: What skills do new employees lack when they first enter the workforce? What recommendations do you have?

LC: Most new employees lack critical thinking skills when they first enter the workforce. They also tend to either lack, or are afraid of, decision-making skills. Some employees enter the team of faculty with a general lack of confidence. It is for this reason that I like to buddy a new person up with an older, more tenured and respected co-worker, at least for the first six months of the new person's employment. In the case of a vocational school, I prefer to have the newer employee work alongside their mentor through one complete cycle of the training program so they have the opportunity to learn how to react in all areas or unusual circumstances.

BK: How can a leader influence and mold the culture of an organization?

LC: A leader can influence and mold the culture of an organization simply by the attitude they expend toward their staff or faculty. If the leader has a positive attitude about the work being performed, the staff will respond to that positivity and work even more diligently to please their leader. Furthermore, a good leader will lead by example and will show their staff that they will not be asked to do something the leader herself would not do. This will encourage loyalty between leadership and staff.

BK: Can organizational politics help an organization?

LC: Organizational politics tend to hurt an organization as far as I am concerned. I have had the opportunity to see this first hand, for example: employees are hired based on who they know, not what they know. This makes for resentment in the team and oftentimes means the team must pick up the slack for the favored staff member. And then of course, team members feel hesitant to complain about that person's lack of productivity for fear of there being serious repercussions. I have learned that in some cases, if one is not a member of the favored inner circle that they will have a difficult time being promoted within the company; though this problem does seem to be alleviated once a larger entity has control of the company.

BK: How important is teamwork in your profession?

LC: Teamwork is the most important aspect of my profession. As a member of a school's faculty we must all work together for solid, positive learning outcomes for our students. Each staff or faculty member must know without a doubt that they have someone willing to jump in and assist them at a moment's notice; this will insure the greater good of all students.

BK: Do you think your education has complemented your work experience or has your work experience complemented your education?

LC: In my case my education has complemented my work experience in that I know that without my Master's in Teaching, I would not have had the opportunity to become a Program Director of a college or a Dean of Education. However, my work experience has also complemented my education because I probably would have been satisfied with my Medical Assisting certificate; it was allowing me to teach at the college. But in 1995 our vocational school was attempting to earn WASC accreditation for the first time. One of the requirements was that all faculties had to have at least an Associate's degree in order to keep their jobs. As long as we were actively working at getting our degrees the school would grandfather us in with a 10% salary increase for each degree we earned. This was a huge motivator for me as I was a single mom supporting my son and had always hoped to attend college but hadn't had the opportunity or financial backing to enroll. You could say I was happily forced into attending college and it was the best decision I ever made for myself.

BK: What motivates you to be successful?

LC: Various things have motivated me to be successful over the years. First and foremost it has always been to prove to my father who passed away when I was 16 years old that I would not waste my life but would work to become a contributing member of society and be successful in my life. Then it was my son and proving to him and me that I could find my way out of the food service industry through hard work and perseverance. Now it has been proving to me that I am still capable of doing anything I set my mind to doing, in spite of various health setbacks.

BK: If you could go back to college, what would you have majored in?

LC: All of my life, from childhood on, I wanted to be a medical doctor. I even went so far as to enlist in the Air Force with my sister when I was 19 years old so that I could get a free education and be trained in the medical field; but on the day we were to be sworn in, I chickened out. So my sister got sworn in, flew a typewriter around Europe for five years, and then earned a Journalism degree from Sacramento State University when she was released from her military obligation. I got married, had a son, and got divorced during those five years she was overseas. I had no college education until I found my vocational school and became a medical assistant in 1989. But based on what I know now and if I would have known how my life was going to progress, I can say that if I had the opportunity to go back to school I would probably work on an MBA. This is certainly not because I like business, but more so because it seems to me that those folks who get their MBA tend to be more successful in today's economy than those like me who went the education route. However, at the same time, I believe that one has to love what they are doing in life so I'm sure that I would still find education to be my first love.

BK: Where do you see yourself in 10 years?

LC: I would like to see myself being the Dean of a college or university in 10 years. I enjoy working in the educational environment and I love to see students when the light bulb of understanding first turns on in their brain! However, in ten years I will be almost retirement age and perhaps I should just say that I would like to be living in England perusing the historical museums, cathedrals, and general stomping grounds of famous writers and educators that came before me!

BK: What is your span of control?

LC: When I was the Program Director of the General Education department my faculty originally was nine strong; but once the department moved to being strictly on-line, I was responsible for two people. When I was the Dean of Education I was in charge of all vocational programs and had a faculty and staff of 40-45 people.

Notes

Amanda Johnson is a Millennial and has seven years of management experience in Higher Education.

BK: Should leaders be more task or relationship oriented?

AJ: I believe that leaders should be more relationship oriented because if sound relationships are made in the workforce, employees will be more inclined to complete their tasks.

BK: Based on your observations, is there still a glass ceiling in the workforce?

AJ: Based on my observations, there is a glass-ceiling in the workforce. As an example, males have higher salaries in the workforce when compared to females. Also, we have more male managers in the workforce than females.

BK: Based on your experiences, what is the best way to manage the different generations in the workforce?

AJ: A manager has to be very careful when managing the different generations in the workforce. Each generation has been influenced by a number of different life events which must be taken into consideration when interacting with them. For example, baby boomers may not have the same technological skills as a millennial or a millennial may not understand the importance of loyalty when compared to a baby boomer.

BK: What generation are you from? What generation/category do the majority of your employees fall under? Has this caused any problems?

AJ: I am a Millennial. The majority of my employees are Generation X'ers and Baby Boomers. It has caused some problems in the workforce. For example, I had to prove myself as a Millennial because I was a lot younger than many of my employees. At times, my employees do not like to take orders from me. Lastly, we have issues based upon productivity levels. As a millennial, I have been raised to be a multitasker but some of my employees refuse to take on a number of different tasks.

BK: As a manager, how do you enhance motivation levels? Please provide some examples/stories.

AJ: To enhance motivational levels, I usually use an incentive such as a one-week paid vacation to Hawaii for two. This usually does the trick because my employees look forward to their vacations. I like to recognize my employees on a regular basis. Lastly, I use a lot of gift cards during meetings and trainings.

BK: What skills/traits do leaders need? How can a person develop his or her leadership skills?

AJ: Leaders today need to have high levels of emotional intelligence skills because employees will perform better when their leader is both understanding and caring. Developing leadership skills takes time. I think that females are better than males because of their innate motherly instincts.

BK: Who is a leader that you admire and why? How has this person influenced your leadership style?

AJ: A leader that I admire is Gandhi. He was a very influential leader and possessed many of the skills that are needed in today's workforce.

BK: Based on your experiences, how has the workforce changed over the years?

AJ: There is more of a dependence on technology which is good and bad. For example, computers help with spelling but I am noticing that many of my employees have difficulties with writing and critical thinking.

BK: What is the difference between management and leadership? What do you consider yourself?

AJ: Management has more to do with focusing on task completion and leadership has more to do with motivating and influencing followers. I think that managers should focus on becoming better leaders.

BK: What kind of performance management system do you use or recommend and why?

AJ: I think using a forced ranking system is helpful to figure out who the strong or average employees are. This also helps determine who the "problem" employees are and helps with determining training needs.

BK: What strategies do you recommend for maximizing productivity levels in the workforce?

AJ: I think that hiring the right people will automatically maximize productivity levels. The recruiting process is very important and should be taken very seriously. It is important that the applicant is a good fit for the organization and the organization is a good fit for the applicant.

BK: Provide some examples of how you empower your employees.

AJ: I like to make sure that my employees are involved in decision making. This is the best way to empower employees.

BK: How do you reward your employees? Should rewards be based on merit?

AJ: From my experiences, rewards should be distributed equally. This will create a culture of teamwork and unity.

BK: What skills do new employees lack when they first enter the workforce? What recommendations do you have?

AJ: New employees who enter the workforce need to enhance their communication skills. I find new employees lack essential communication skills that are needed when presenting information or writing a memo.

BK: How can a leader influence and mold the culture of an organization?

AJ: This is not an easy process. Leaders need to understand that an organization's culture is very sacred and both leaders and employees need to work together to mold a sustainable culture.

BK: Can organizational politics help an organization?

AJ: Organizational politics will not help an organization. Unfortunately, the majority of organizations use politics to create allies and enemies. This practice is both toxic and unjust. Employees prefer transparency, equality, and accountability.

BK: How important is teamwork in your profession?

AJ: Teamwork is very important in my profession. I encourage my employees to work in teams because teams are able to produce better projects. I am a firm believer that two or more brains work better than one.

BK: Do you think your education has complemented your work experience or has your work experience complemented your education?

AJ: I strongly believe that my education has complemented my work experience. An education without significant work experience can be detrimental.

BK: What motivates you to be successful?

AJ: I am motivated to be successful because my goal is to be able to help others be successful. Ultimately, I need to be successful in order to help others.

BK: If you could go back to college, what would you have majored in?

AJ: If I could go back to college, I would study Business Administration with an emphasis in Management.

BK: Where do you see yourself in 10 years?

AJ: In ten years, I hope to be in a top management position.

BK: What is your span of control?

AJ: My span of control is 12 employees.

Notes

Diane Cvetic is a Baby Boomer and has 11 years of management experience in Higher Education.

BK: Should leaders be more task or relationship oriented?

DC: Leaders should manage to their strengths, which in turn will determine whether they should be more task or relationship oriented. A leader who is task oriented by nature should embrace the benefits of focusing on getting things done and delegate the relationship oriented issues to someone on the team who prefers relationship oriented processes. The leader who prefers a more relationship oriented leadership style will find it easy to spot those members of the team who are more task-oriented and tap into their strengths for the benefit of the entire team.

BK: Based on your observations, is there still a glass ceiling in the workforce?

DC: Even though I know the glass ceiling still exists, I have not observed it in my most recent role as a manager. Both women and minorities (and women minorities) have been in top-level management positions in the post-secondary education companies I have worked for in the past 18 years.

BK: Based on your experiences, what is the best way to manage the different generations in the workforce?

DC: Rather than grouping employees into categories based on their generation, I tend to look at each employee as a unique and valuable individual who might be strongly or weakly influenced by their generational peers. When conflicts arise that appear to be based on generational differences, I try to focus on the problem rather than focusing on the differences among workers based on age.

BK: What generation are you from? What generation/category do the majority of your employees fall under? Has this caused any problems?

DC: I am a Baby Boomer (barely!) The majority of my employees have been from the same generation. This has not caused any problems working together but because many of the students are from Generations X and Y, we have had to adjust to younger students acting more entitled than we did at their age.

BK: As a manager, how do you enhance motivation levels? Please provide some examples/stories.

DC: One of the things I do to enhance motivation levels in my employees is to discuss how the work they are doing is of measurable value to the organization. Everyone needs to know that their contributions at work are of value. I remember one time how upset one of my employees was when I failed to include her in the process of developing and presenting a faculty in-service presentation. I had no idea that it was such an important thing to her until I thoughtlessly (albeit unintentionally) did not invite her to participate in the presentation.

I prefer to help my employees develop their own intrinsic motivation rather than rely solely on extrinsic incentives for work accomplished at a predetermined level of acceptability. To foster intrinsic motivation, I make sure that my employees have the opportunity to engage in creative problem solving, and I never force them to "make it rain on Tuesday" or face negative consequences if something beyond their control does not happen as expected.

I also listen carefully to my employees to learn what motivates them so that I can clearly define my methods for rewarding and recognizing accomplishments in order to enhance motivation levels.

BK: What skills/traits do leaders need? How can a person develop his or her leadership skills?

DC: Leaders must have a clear mission, a clear vision, values, and both long and short term goals, but more importantly, they must be competent followers as well. This means that they must have superb active listening skills, a healthy working relationship with everyone on the team, and the insight into knowing when team members should take the lead in projects and why.

One step in the process of developing leadership skills is to select one or more well- known leaders that display admirable leadership abilities and try out some of the methods they use to see how they "fit". It is important to assess and self-reflect for the purpose of revising and improving leadership strategies as needed to reach optimum performance as a leader.

BK: Who is a leader that you admire and why? How has this person influenced your leadership style?

DC: I admire Warren Buffet. His approach makes sense to me, and I like the fact that he treats business like a fascinating challenge rather than a corrupt game in which you can discard your personal values if they get in the way of making money. His approach has influenced my leadership style at work and in my own business. By treating my business like a challenge with rules rather than a money making endeavor in which exploiting others for the purpose of financial gain is expected, I have succeeded both financially and personally.

BK: Based on your experiences, how has the workforce changed over the years?

DC: The workforce feels more employee-focused than when I took my first job in the early 1980s. In other words, employees seem more empowered to speak up and be heard. On the other hand, there seems to be a lot less loyalty. Very few people expect to have just one job for the entire span of their career.

BK: What is the difference between management and leadership? What do you consider yourself?

DC: Management is about controlling performance; leadership is about empowering people to achieve optimal performance. I prefer being a leader; although, I have found myself in management mode more often than I would like.

BK: What kind of performance management system do you use or recommend and why?

DC: I recommend a performance management system that engages the employee in the process of self-reflection of performance and setting measurable goals for continuous improvement. I am not a fan of the "stack ranking" systems and would never recommend using them.

BK: What strategies do you recommend for maximizing productivity levels in the workforce?

DC: Empowering employees to be part of the process of determining how to maximize productivity is essential to achieving maximum productivity. People do not typically like being told what they need to do to become more productive. When given the freedom to get creative about challenging themselves, employees typically rise to the occasion and are more satisfied in their work.

BK: Provide some examples of how you empower your employees.

DC: I empower my employees by providing a work environment in which their input and ideas are valued. I encourage them to brainstorm ideas for solving problems that prevent us from reaching optimal productivity. I also encourage them to propose new procedures or ideas. I have often asked employees to think about what they would do if they owned the company.

BK: How do you reward your employees? Should rewards be based on merit?

DC: I know that employees need to be recognized for their accomplishments, but I'm not in favor of rewarding expected behaviors or accomplishments unless it's a mundane task that no one wants to do. In those limited situations, a small reward for getting to the end of the boring assignment can help employees stay motivated. The academic organizations that I have worked for base annual salary increases on merit, so I encourage my employees to set goals for the year and then show me how their achievements have contributed to the success of the department and ultimately the organization. I also use data collected throughout the year to help support my decision on the amount of merit pay increase each employee receives.

BK: What skills do new employees lack when they first enter the workforce? What recommendations do you have?

DC: Many employees entering the workforce for the first time lack the fine-tuned skills of acclimating to the political environment of the workplace. They come in with certain expectations about how everyone should treat each other, and when those expectations are not met, they can get rather upset and handle their frustrations and other negative emotions ineffectively.

BK: How can a leader influence and mold the culture of an organization?

DC: An effective leader provides the framework for both influencing and molding the culture of an organization. Every action (and reaction) of the leader that is observed by employees helps mold the organizational culture, so it is important for the leader to take advantage of this by engaging in purposeful, intentional behaviors toward creating the ideal culture.

BK: Can organizational politics help an organization?

DC: Yes. Once we understand that organizational politics is a normal phenomenon based on normal human social behaviors regarding power, we can use organizational politics to help the organization achieve its goals. Leaders are developed in organizations based on the ways in which they engage effectively in organizational politics.

BK: How important is teamwork in your profession?

DC: Effective teamwork is essential in for-profit post-secondary education. Not only must members of a department team work effectively together, but interdepartmental teams must interact to create meta-teams that must also be able to work effectively together.

BK: Do you think your education has complemented your work experience or has your work experience complemented your education?

DC: I think it is a little bit of each. My undergraduate education in psychology complemented my work as a post-secondary instructor, and later, my graduate work in education was complemented by my work as Dean and Program Director.

BK: What motivates you to be successful?

DC: I am intrinsically motivated to succeed. I stay engaged in workplace challenges just to see if I can come up with a viable solution. I am not too motivated by money, promotions, and raises, but I need to make enough to keep a roof over my head. Once that level has been met, I do not need the "carrot" dangled in front of me to get me motivated. I need challenges that have possible solutions. There is nothing more demotivating than being asked to do the verifiably impossible.

BK: If you could go back to college, what would you have majored in?

DC: I would not have done anything differently. I loved the undergraduate work I did in Psychology and the graduate work I did in Education.

BK: Describe a typical day at work for you.

DC: Each day is different for me. Most of what I do involves solving problems. Most of the problems involve helping people overcome challenges or discovering new information to solve a perplexing problem.

BK: Where do you see yourself in 10 years?

DC: I hope to still be working in post-secondary education. I have recently left a vocational college and taken a position in a university and I hope to take on more and more responsibilities as I become more experienced in this new academic setting.

BK: What is your span of control?

DC: I have managed as many as eight Program Directors as Dean and eight Instructors as Program Director.

Notes

Pam Whitehouse is a Baby Boomer and has 10 years of management experience in Higher Education.

BK: Should leaders be more task or relationship oriented?

PW: In order to be a great leader you have to have both task and relationship orientated skills. They both are very important for leadership success. You need to be able to keep up with all tasks that are required. I would also add that a leader that has strong relationships with staff or employees creates a better and stronger work environment. As a result, employees have a feeling of being heard, recognized, and appreciated.

BK: Based on your observations, is there still a glass ceiling in the workforce?

PW: In my observations, I have not seen this glass ceiling when dealing with women or minorities in becoming top-level managers.

BK: Based on your experiences, what is the best way to manage the different generations in the workforce?

PW: As a manager of different generations you need to understand their generation. You need to be open to new ideas but also be able to control and benefit from different ideas and thoughts.

BK: What generation are you from? What generation/category do the majority of your employees fall under? Has this caused any problems?

PW: I am a Baby Boomer. As the Dean of Academic Affairs, I managed all categories: Baby Boomers, Generations X and Y. I would say some of the challenges that I experienced are different levels of work ethic, the drive to succeed in career, and the drive to meet the requirements of the position. I have found the most difficult group to manage is the Generation Y. My experience is that they have low levels of work ethic. They seemed to not take their positions as serious as they should have. With the Baby Boomers, I noticed that they seemed to have difficulty with changes in processes and management and would respond with pushback.

BK: As a manager, how do you enhance motivation levels? Please provide some examples/stories.

PW: I would try to encourage employees or motivate them with small rewards and recognition. In the education field, I would always remind them of the success they are creating for their students. In the retail arena, I have come up with rewards for promoting products or upgrading sales. Because this is a new adventure for me in retail, my rewards are small. Currently, I will buy them lunch for a good day.

BK: What skills/traits do leaders need? How can a person develop his or her leadership skills?

PW: Skills for leaders would be: strong communicator, good listener, multitasker, promote growth, fair, and professional. These skills and others can be taught through training.

BK: Who is a leader that you admire and why? How has this person influenced your leadership style?

PW: I admire my first boss in the education field. She shared her knowledge and helped me be a good educator. She influenced me to further my own education and to always strive for more. As a leader, she was a good listener, fair, and assisted me in my own personal growth.

BK: Based on your experiences, how has the workforce changed over the years?

PW: Over the years, I would say work ethic and values don't seem to be the same. Today, it is harder to find the right person for the job.

BK: What is the difference between management and leadership? What do you consider yourself?

PW: Management is the "higher ups" which could be your leaders as well, but your co-worker can be a leader as well. Hopefully, you have leaders in your management group. I consider myself both. Being in management you should be a leader as well.

BK: What kind of performance management system do you use or recommend and why?

PW: In my role as the Dean, we would use a unique performance evaluation method that was fair to all employees.

BK: What strategies do you recommend for maximizing productivity levels in the workforce?

PW: I always encourage employees to meet, if not exceed expectations. The organization has awards for employees exceeding benchmarks so this is a driving force for some employees. I also set expectations or tasks that needed to be completed by deadlines that I provided for them.

BK: Provide some examples of how you empower your employees.

PW: I managed Program Directors; it has many job duties that require them to make decisions. I would encourage them to make the best decisions for their departments. I put trust in them. I would always be available to assist them if they needed it.

BK: How do you reward your employees? Should rewards be based on merit?

PW: As a manager I could reward my employees with lunches, quarterly awards, and corporate reward programs. I feel if the employee is meeting or exceeding the job description, they are eligible for rewards.

BK: What skills do new employees lack when they first enter the workforce? What recommendations do you have?

PW: In my experience they lack: work ethic, professionalism, and customer service. I would recommend that all new hires have a strong understanding of these expectations before being hired.

BK: How can a leader influence and mold the culture of an organization?

PW: I would have to say trust, honesty, and believing in the mission statement. In my earlier days in education I had a leader that built trust and was honest with all the staff. He created a compassionate, caring and successful campus. All employees were proud of what they did.

BK: Can organizational politics help an organization?

PW: NO! I feel it creates a mess.

BK: How important is teamwork in your profession?

PW: I feel teamwork is important in most professions when a difficult problem needs to be solved.

BK: Do you think your education has complemented your work experience or has your work experience complemented your education?

PW: I would have to say a little of both.

BK: What motivates you to be successful?

PW: Initially it was to show my family I could do it. As I moved up in positions it was my co-workers. They encouraged me to continue with my education and to seek higher positions.

BK: If you could go back to college, what would you have majored in?

PW: Psychology because everything relates to psychology.

BK: Describe a typical day at work for you.

PW: Assisting managers with student issues, working with the Executive Director and Registrar, dealing with student issues, and preparing reports for upper management.

BK: Where do you see yourself in 10 years?

PW: Preparing for retirement.

BK: What is your span of control?

PW: Over 50 employees.

Notes

Summary

Chapter 9 provides ten exclusive interviews with managers from different generations. Each manager has a unique philosophy on organizational issues. The interviewees also provided valuable knowledge for future leaders and managers based upon their vast experiences.

Chapter Review Questions

1. Which interview can you relate to the most? Explain why.

2. Create a table highlighting the demographics (e.g., number of interviewees, gender, generation, education, management experience, span of control, etc.) of this group of managers. After creating the table, what correlations do you see?

3. Did you notice any similarities/differences among the Millennial responses? Did you notice any similarities/differences among the Generation X responses? Did you notice any similarities/differences among the Baby Boomer responses? Explain your findings.

4. Why is it difficult to manage a multi-generational workforce? Provide some recommendations as to how a multigenerational workforce should be managed.

5. Did you notice any similarities/differences among the male responses? Explain your findings.

6. Did you notice any similarities/differences among the female responses? Explain your findings.

7. Did you notice a correlation between management experience and management philosophy? Explain your findings.

8. What did you find to be the most interesting about the interviews?

9. Do you think that your management philosophy has been influenced as a result of reading and analyzing these interviews? Justify your response.

10. Do you think quantitative or qualitative research is more meaningful? Justify your response.

10

The Future of Organizations

Managing and leading organizations of the future will be difficult because of the following: globalization, a multigenerational workforce, dependency on technology, unethical behaviors and practices (e.g., Enron's decision to ignore illegal accounting practices), and many other factors. Moreover, managers will have to learn how to effectively deal with employees who have a Machiavellian mentality of "doing whatever it takes to get his or her own way" in every situation. In addition, managers will need to learn how to manage a diverse workforce also known as diversity management. Interestingly enough, "Half of the PhDs working in the United States are foreign-born" (Fisher, 2002). Diversity management can simply be defined as effectively embracing, promoting, and managing differences in the workforce. It is important to mention that diversity management is not only about race and ethnicity but also encompasses religion, sexual orientation, values, age, marital status, gender, and myriad other variables. If an organization does not take diversity management seriously, it can end up in a multimillion dollar law suit like Denny's Restaurants, Coca-Cola, and

Home Depot. In 1994, Denny's Restaurants suffered a public relations disaster and paid $54 million to settle discrimination lawsuits. Coca-Cola settled a class action suit by African American employees for $192 million in November 2000. "Home Depot paid $104 million to settle a gender lawsuit" (Mujtaba, 2010, p. 8). Denny's Restaurants' transformation was so drastic that the company has regularly been at or near the top spot on Fortune's list of the fifty best companies for minorities (Esposito et al., 2002). As a result, organizations have started regular diversity trainings to help employees understand the importance of diversity in the workforce.

Multi-Generational Workforce

Over the past sixty years, there have been three generations, the Baby Boomer Generation, Generation X, and most currently Generation Y, also known as "Millennials". Interestingly enough, "organizations and researchers are just now beginning to address issues related to generational differences that may have a significant impact on the leadership and success of the organization" (Salahuddin, 2010, p. 1). It becomes imperative to learn as much about the Millennial generation as possible. Baby Boomers are starting to retire, and as a result, more Millennials are being hired throughout the nation. As such, the differences among the generations in the workforce can create problems for managers who are responsible for making sure that tasks are being completed. Consequently, differences "create problems among team members that ultimately result in reduced effectiveness" (Colquitt, Lepine, & Wesson, 2011, p. 392). Table 14 depicts the three different generations currently in the workforce and when they were born.

Three Generations in the Workforce
Table 14

Generation	Date of Birth
Baby Boomers	1946-1964
Generation X	1965-1980
Generation Y or Millennials	After 1980

In order to correctly understand Millennials, it becomes imperative to also understand their more experienced counterparts. As mentioned above, Baby Boomers were born between the years 1946-1964, and are the largest group (representing approximately 79 million in the US) of the three generations (Rosenberg, 2009).

Baby Boomers

After World War II, young males returned home and started families resulting in a large number of new babies (baby boom) (Rosenberg, 2009). Baby Boomers who were born in the United States were raised in a prosperous economic time. Baby Boomers are optimists who grew up expecting the world to progress and for the wars to end. After some of their icons were assassinated (e.g., Martin Luther King and the Kennedy brothers), this generation rejected traditional norms and values. Furthermore, this generation did not grow up dependent on technology. As a result, they view technology as "artifacts" of organizational culture (Simons, 2010, p. 31). In regards to understanding this group, Baby Boomers possess traits that are shared among the members of other generations. Baby Boomers enjoy having the autonomy to focus on some of their own hobbies (e.g., playing golf, gardening, volunteering, and just relaxing). The majority of Baby Boomers prefer having flexible work options, acknowledge the importance of work/life balance, and prefer to work remotely. Furthermore, Baby Boomers like to volunteer and help keep this planet healthy (Hewlett et al., 2009, p. 73). "The Baby Boomers are also one of the most educated generations" (Colquitt, Lepine, & Wesson, 2011, p. 85). As the Baby Boomer Generation prepares for retirement, the next generation (Generation X) will be taking over many of these positions.

Generation X (a.k.a. Gen X)

According to Kane (2012), "Generation X encompasses the 44 to 50 million Americans born between 1965 and 1980. This generation marks the period of birth decline after the baby boom and is significantly smaller than previous and succeeding generations." This generation has unique traits. For example, they are often described as "individualistic, risk-tolerant, self-reliant, entrepreneurial, comfortable with diversity, and valuing work-life balance" (Gentry et al., 2011, p. 39). Generation X managers will typically be less formal, and more adaptable than their predecessors. Gen Xers tend to focus on outcomes rather than the process (Dols et al., 2010, p. 69). Other researchers have concluded that this generation lacks people skills. "For Gen X managers, the trait of independence comes with negatives: being impatient, having poor people skills, and working from a place of cynicism. They are also very straightforward and tend to lack people skills, which may affect employee retention" (Salahuddin, 2010, p. 4). As managers, this generation uses a contingent based style depending on the situation that they are facing. In one study, Generation X managers "labeled their leadership as situational" as opposed to Boomers who practiced servant leadership (Salahuddin, 2010, p. 5). When given a task to complete, Gen Xers prefer instructions such as, "do it your way" and "there aren't a lot of rules" because of their self-reliance. As leaders, they utilize the same [laissez-faire] style (Gentry, 2011, p. 45). The next generation has proven to be a powerful force in the organization because of their technological proficiencies.

Generation Y (a.k.a. Millennials)

Millennials have grown up in the digital age. They show greater familiarity than previous generations with communication, media, and digital technologies. Millennials are more "wired" which gives them a competitive advantage and makes them an asset when it comes to working with new technologies. However, Tolbzie (2008) points out that, "they are also sometimes called the "Trophy Generation" or "Trophy Kids" based on the emerging trend in sports and competition to reward everyone for participation, rather than for winning" (p.12). For this reason, Millennials have been known to reject in-house competition and politics. Furthermore, because many watched their parents be adversely affected by the Dot-com bubble burst and high rates of divorce and layoffs, Millennials are thought to be skeptical of long-term commitments, and are said to desire greater flexibility in their career. Members of this generation are described as preferring collective action, working in teams, wanting work that really matters to them, and being civic-minded, eco-aware, confident, conventional, optimistic, and socially conscious (Hewlett et al., 2009). One research study described Millennials as "opinionated" and they "[expect] to be heard" (Hartman & McCambridge, 2011, p. 24). As such, the goal should be to learn more about Millennials because they will be leading organizations of the future.

Use of Teams

Organizations will continue to depend more on teams than individuals for completing complex projects. The team approach has many benefits because it provides for a larger pool of knowledge. The Tuckman Model, named after Bruce Tuckman (1965), provides a framework for understanding team development. According to the model, there are five stages of team development: forming, storming, norming, performing, and adjourning. The forming stage is when teammates get to know each other and try to understand their boundaries among the team. The storming stage is when ideas are exchanged (brainstorming) triggering some disagreement and unwanted tension. The norming stage is when teammates understand that they need to work together to complete their task and norms are established. The performing stage is when the team works together to accomplish their goal. The adjourning stage is when team members disengage and separate from the team. Figure 28 on the next page illustrates the team development process.

The Tuckman Model
Figure 28

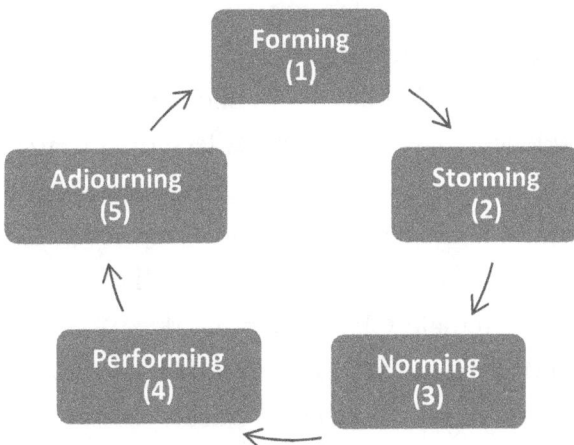

One potential setback to the use of teams is a concept known as groupthink. Groupthink can be defined as, "a deterioration of mental efficiency, reality testing, and moral judgment resulting from pressures within the group" (Nelson & Quick, 2011, p. 346). A famous example of groupthink is NASA's 1986 decision to forcefully launch the space shuttle Challenger in unusually cold weather and with unstable O-rings which resulted in a major tragedy. On the eve of the launch, an emergency teleconference had been called between NASA and the Morton Thiokol Corporation. "During the teleconference, Thiokol engineers pleaded with supervisors and NASA to delay the launch. They feared cold temperatures would cause a failure in synthetic rubber O-rings sealing the rocket motor's joints. If the rings failed, the motor could blow up" (Bolman & Deal, 2008, p. 192). It was later concluded that flawed decision making was the primary cause of the accident. As such, the goal should be to learn how teams can work collectively on projects without being influenced by groupthink and organizational politics.

Gender Equality in the Workforce

Managers who will be leading organizations of the future should consider the importance of gender equality in the workforce. "In gender studies of public administration, there is significant evidence that women have less organizational power than men, measured in lower pay, fewer career opportunities, and underrepresentation at the highest leadership levels" (Portillo & Dehart-Davis, 2009, p. 339). Furthermore, "Despite high-profile success stories of female CEOs such as Meg Whitman of eBay, only a handful of Fortune 500 firms in 2008 have a woman in the top spot. Consequently, concern remains about the progress women are making" (Wyld, 2008, p. 83). Many believe that the glass ceiling has been shattered for women and minorities; however, evidence exists that there still is a significant amount of inequality in the workforce. "The glass ceiling is a concept popularized in the 1980s to describe a barrier so subtle that it is transparent, yet so strong that it prevents women and minorities from moving up in the management hierarchy" (Morrison & Glinow, 1995, p. 169). The following figure shows the anticipated first-year salaries of male and female undergraduates (Casserly, 2012). As seen below, males make approximately 15% more than their female counterparts.

Gender and First-Year Salaries
Figure 29

Undergrad Expected annual salary (USD)

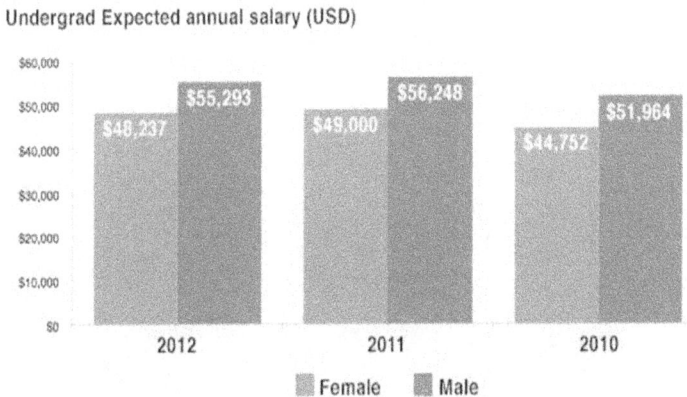

	2012	2011	2010
Female	$48,237	$49,000	$44,752
Male	$55,293	$56,248	$51,964

Female   Male

As a different example, female executives in healthcare earn significantly lower salaries than male executives. "The male-female salary gap, adjusting for education and experience/time in the workforce, has been stable over time: men earned 18 percent more than women in 1990, 17 percent more in 1995, 19 percent more in 2000, and 18 percent more in 2006. In 2006, nearly one third (29 percent) of women said they did not receive fair compensation because of gender, compared to only 1 percent of men" (Lantz, 2008, p. 292). As such, the goal should be to create a workforce that promotes and values gender equality.

The New Generation of Managing and Leadership Organizations

The new generation of managing and leading organizations will require individuals to have specific traits that will assist them in their professions. More specifically, managers and leaders need to be intelligent so they can conceptualize complex situations, but more importantly, they need other key traits in order to be successful in the future. For example, they need innate emotional intelligence skills, instinctive cultural intelligence competencies, and genuine positive intelligence inclinations. As such, the goal should be to develop managers and leaders with high levels of positive intelligence, cultural intelligence, and emotional intelligence. Figure 30 illustrates this model for future managers and leaders.

Management and Leadership Competency Model
Figure 30

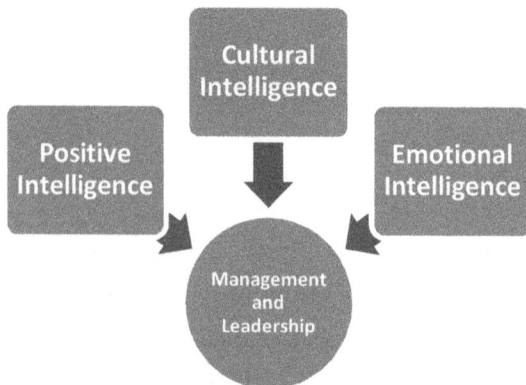

Positive Intelligence

Positive intelligence is an important trait to have in all situations. Unfortunately, most people do not understand the implications of being positive in the workforce. According to Achor (2012), "Research shows that when people work with a positive mindset, performance on nearly every level—productivity, creativity, engagement—improves. Yet happiness is perhaps the most misunderstood driver of performance" (p. 100). Interestingly enough, "Most people think that success proceeds happiness" (Achor, 2012, p. 100). In reality, happiness produces success. As a practical example, some employees believe the following, "Once I get a promotion, I'll be happy." Research has shown that if an employee is happy, he or she will perform at higher levels and as a result will be more inclined to get a promotion. In fact, in a sweeping meta-analysis of 225 academic studies reported in *Harvard Business Review*, researchers found that "happy employees are, on average, 31% more productive. Their sales are also 37% higher, and their creativity is three times higher" (Achor, 2012, p. 102). Therefore, it is important for managers and leaders to be able to develop new habits by training one's brain to be positive. It is also important to help coworkers because in a study of 1,648 Harvard students "social support was the greatest predictor of happiness during periods of high stress" (pp. 101-102). Achor (2012) continues, "employees who score the highest on providing social support, are 40% more likely to receive a promotion in the following year, report significantly higher job satisfaction, and feel ten times more engaged by their jobs than people who score in the lowest quartile" (p. 102). Finally, it should be mentioned that changing one's relationship with stress can help with having a positive mindset. Stress should be strategically used as a means of motivation because "stress is just not an obstacle to growth; it can be the fuel for it" (Achor, 2012, p. 102). In other words, your professional growth relates to your attitude toward stress.

Cultural Intelligence

Cultural intelligence resides in the body (physical), heart (emotional/motivational), and head (cognitive). Earley and Moaskowsk (2004) explain, "Occasionally an outsider has a seemingly natural ability to interpret someone's unfamiliar and ambiguous gestures in just the way that that person's compatriots and colleagues would, even to mirror them. We call that cultural intelligence" and the authors further state, "In a world where crossing boundaries is routine, cultural intelligence becomes a vitally important aptitude and skill, and not just for international bankers and borrowers" (p. 139). Cultural intelligence is developed through emotional and motivational means by having confidence to understand, embrace, and adapt to a new culture. In addition, cultural intelligence is developed through cognitive means by observing, critically analyzing, and learning about other cultures. Finally, cultural intelligence is developed through physical means by using senses and adapting movements to blend in. As a practical example, it is very common in many cultures to kiss and hug when greeting one another, while in other cultures it is disrespectful to show familiarity to a person by touching them. Also, it is common in some cultures to stand (as a sign of respect and acknowledgement) when someone enters your office. As a case in point, in the movie, *The Karate Kid* (Part 2), young Daniel LaRusso decides to travel to Okinawa, Japan with his sensei (karate teacher and mentor) Mr. Miyagi. While on his trip, Daniel has to develop his cultural intelligence competencies in order to adapt to his new environment.

By understanding and embracing other cultures, it becomes easier to manage a diverse group of employees. A great way to learn about other cultures is to travel to different parts of the world. If traveling is not an option, it can be as a simple as having conversations with people from different cultures. There are books that can also be a great resource for managers and leaders who understand the importance of cultural intelligence in the workforce. Managers can also ask their employees to hold monthly cultural awareness trainings, seminars, interviews, and also workshops. The following survey (Figure 31) allows an individual to assess his or her cultural intelligence levels.

Cultural Intelligence Survey
Figure 31

Cultural Intelligence Survey		
Developed by P. Christopher Earley and Elaine Mosakowski (2004)		
These statements reflect different facets of cultural intelligence. For each set, add up your scores and divide by four to produce an average. Research with large groups of managers shows that for purposes of your own development, it is most useful to think about your three scores in comparison to one another. Generally, an average of less than 3 would indicate an area calling for improvement, while an average greater than 4.5 reflects true cultural intelligence strength. Rate the extent to which you agree with each statement using the scale:		
1 = strongly disagree, 2 = disagree, 3 = neutral, 4 = agree, 5 = strongly agree		
	Before I interact with people from a new culture, I ask myself what I hope to achieve.	
	If I encounter something unexpected while working in a new culture, I use this experience to figure out new ways to approach other cultures in the future.	
	I plan how I am going to relate to people from a different culture before I meet them.	
	When I come in to a new cultural situation, I can immediately sense whether something is going well or something is going wrong.	
Total:	Total_____ /4 = _____ **Cognitive Cultural Intelligence**	
	It is easy for me to change my body language (for example, eye contact or posture) to suit people from a different culture.	
	I can alter my expression when a cultural encounter requires it.	
	I modify my speech style (for example, accent or tone) to suit people from a different culture.	
	I easily change the way I act when a cross-cultural encounter seems to require it.	
Total:	Total_____/4 = _____ **Physical Cultural Intelligence**	
	I have confidence that I can deal well with people from a different culture.	
	I am certain that I can befriend people whose cultural backgrounds are different from mine.	
	I can adapt to the lifestyle of a different culture with relative ease.	
	I am confident that I can deal with an unfamiliar cultural situation.	
Total:	Total_____/4=_____ **Motivational Cultural Intelligence**	

Emotional Intelligence

Since it was first suggested by Salovey and Mayer (1990), emotional intelligence has been a topic of great interest to scientists researching non-cognitive factors that may contribute to intelligence. As mentioned above, emotional intelligence is the ability to identify, assess, and control the emotions of oneself, of others, and of groups. Emotional intelligence as a paradigm was further developed by Goleman (1996, 1999). It is often suggested that people equipped with emotional intelligence have a competitive edge in both their personal and professional lives and as a result, are happier and more successful (Murphy & Janeke, 2009). While the subject of emotional intelligence in recent decades has become an area of much study and debate, it should be noted that the underlying concepts of emotional intelligence are not entirely new ideas, and in fact, have a history dating to the nineteenth century. The work of the English naturalist, Charles Darwin, emphasized the role of emotional expression in survival and adaptation.

Interestingly enough, "Many believe that there is a human ability that affects social functioning, called emotional intelligence" (Colquitt, et al., p. 347). "Although emotional intelligence is now part of the vocabulary in most organizations, few leaders we've worked with are fully comfortable engaging their own emotions or managing the emotions of others" (Schwartz, et al., 2010, pp. 123-124). Robbins and Coulter (2005) explain that "emotional intelligence is an assortment of non-cognitive skills, capabilities, and competencies that influence a person's ability to succeed in coping with environmental demands and pressures" (p. 355).

Controlling personal feelings is a skill that allows an individual to perceive and better address the emotions of those around them. Furthermore, detecting shifts in the emotions of colleagues is an important first step to transforming attitudes from negative to positive. For example, in a business context, high emotional intelligence is demonstrated to have roles in both moderating conflict resolution and enhancing organizational citizenship behavior (Salami, 2010).Whatever the leadership style, emotional intelligence enables a leader to create interpersonal trust and improve communication, thereby increasing "workplace climate and business outcomes" (Rao, 2006, p. 316).

Emotional intelligence development will allow a leader to recognize emotions immediately and respond by promoting a positive mood to maintain constructive performance. Furthermore, people with high emotional intelligence can generally balance multiple tasks without losing sight of priorities, have the ability to solve new problems in unique and creative ways, and work well in group-oriented tasks (Murphy & Janeke, 2009). In addition, leaders with emotional intelligence are able to recognize and control their personal emotions and may benefit from lower levels of anger.

Summary

Chapter 10 discussed the future of organizations and the challenges that managers and leaders will face. For example, managers and leaders will have to focus on a multi-generational workforce, the use of teams, and gender equality in the workforce. This chapter also addressed the importance of managers and leaders developing new skills in order to be effective. A number of examples were used to help illustrate key points.

Conclusion

As organizations continue to evolve, the future will require managers and leaders to continuously update their skills, education/trainings, and understanding of managing and leading a diverse workforce. Furthermore, managers and leaders will need to figure out the optimum way of influencing their followers by using their power. According to John French and Bertram Raven (1959), there are five types of power: legitimate, reward, expert, referent, and coercive. Legitimate power is the belief that a person has the right to make demands, and expect compliance and obedience from others; while reward power results from one person's ability to compensate another for compliance. Expert power is based on a person's superior skill and knowledge, while referent power is the result of a person's perceived attractiveness, worthiness, and right to respect from others. And finally, coercive power comes from the belief that a person can punish others for noncompliance. There is no magical recipe to treat all organizations (i.e., contingency theory) but over the years many theories, constructs, and models have been developed (that are mentioned in this book) to help organizations continuously evolve. Understanding organizational behavior can help employees, managers, and leaders become more successful in the workforce.

Chapter Review Questions

1. Why can a Machiavellian mentality be toxic in an organization?

2. What are the benefits of hiring a diverse workforce? What does diversity management mean to you?

3. As Baby Boomers retire, what can employees from Generation X and Generation Y learn from them?

4. How can groupthink be avoided when working in teams? What are some other examples of groupthink in our society?

5. Do you agree with Tuckman's Model of team development? Justify your response.

6. How can stress help an employee become more successful?

7. Why is positive intelligence so important? How do you use positive intelligence in your daily life?

8. Why is cultural intelligence so important? Where do you learn the majority of your information about different cultures? How accurate is the information?

9. Why is emotional intelligence so important? Do you think that females have higher emotional intelligence levels than males? Justify your response.

10. How did you score on the cultural intelligence survey? Why do you think you earned this score?

Discussion Questions

1. Do you think that it is good or bad that Millennials will be leading organizations of the future? Justify your response. What can organizations do to learn more about Millennials?

2. How can teams work collectively on projects without being influenced by groupthink and organizational politics? What strategies would you implement?

3. What can be done to ensure that organizations promote and value gender equality?

4. What can be done to develop managers and leaders with high levels of positive intelligence, cultural intelligence, and emotional intelligence?

Case Study

Larry is a manager at *XYZ Solutions*, which is a management consulting firm. The firm has a number of employees who graduated from various Ivy League schools. The employees have extremely high IQ levels and have been very successful in helping American corporations with managerial issues. Recently, a number of international clients from Brazil, Russia, India, and China (BRIC countries with emerging economies) have requested assistance. Larry recognizes that his employees have never traveled internationally and is cautious about sending any of his employees overseas for consulting purposes. He decides to hold a meeting with his employees. At the meeting, it becomes clear that most of his Ivy League "hot shots" are confident that they will be just as successful in the BRIC countries. Larry finally agrees to send three of his senior consultants to India. Of the three senior consultants, two are Baby Boomers and one is a Millennial. The two Baby Boomers are not really thrilled (pessimistic) about going to India and leaving their families behind for a month but are forced to go by Larry. The Millennial is excited to go with the two senior consultants because her ultimate goal is to become a senior consultant and she will soon need recommendations and support from the senior consultants. All she has to do is agree with the senior consultants (not challenge the status quo) and everything will be fine. The three leave for India and safely arrive.

Two weeks later, Larry receives a call from an Indian manager complaining about the consultants. The Indian manager asserts, "They do not understand our culture, our values, and our way of life." Larry is astonished and tells the Indian manager that he will call him back. Larry quickly decides to call his friend who is an "organizational development doctor" to analyze and diagnose this situation.

Case Questions

1. What questions should the organizational development doctor ask Larry? What questions should be asked of the three consultants?

2. Was it a bad idea to send the two Baby Boomers and why?

3. Was it a bad idea to send the Millennial and why?

4. Was it a bad idea to send consultants overseas with no international experience, why?

5. Conduct a RED Analysis on this case and explain your findings.

Special Case Assignment

Select a BRIC country and create a 10-minute presentation explaining the culture of the country. Your presentation should serve as a foundational training for future consultants who go to that country. You should consider doing some outside research on Geert Hofstede's Dimensions of Cultural Values.

BIBLIOGRAPHY

Abhishek, S., Locke, E. A, & Bartol, K. M. (2001). Money and Subjective Well-Being: It's Not the Money, it's the Motives. *Journal of Personality and Social Psychology*, 80(6), 959-971.

Abrahamson, E. (1996). Management Fashion. *Academy of Management Review*, 21(1), 254-285.

Abrahamson, E. (1997). The Emergence and Prevalence of Employee Management Rhetorics: The Effects of Long Waves, Labor Unions, and Turnover, 1875-1992. *Academy of Management Journal*, 40, 491-533.

Achor, S. (2012). Positive Intelligence. *Harvard Business Review*, January-February 2012, 100-102.

Adams, J.S. (1965). Inequity in Social Exchange. *Advances in Experimental Social Psychology*, 62, 335-343.

Allen. T.D., & Rush, M.C. (1998). The Effects of Organizational Citizenship Behavior on Performance Judgments: A Field Study and a Laboratory Experiment. *Journal of Applied Psychology*, 83, 247-260.

Anderson, J. C., Rungtusanatham, M., & Schroeder, R. G. (1994). A Theory of Quality Management Underlying the Deming Management Method. *Academy of Management Review*, 19(3), 472-509.

Argyris, C., & Payne, M. (1995, October). *Organizational Learning II: Theory, Method, and Practice*. Reading, MA: Addison Wesley Longman, Inc.

Argyris, C., & Schon, D. A. (1992, January). *Theory in Practice: Increasing Professional Effectiveness*. San Francisco, CA: Josey-Bass Publishers.

Azalea, A., Omar, F., & Mastor, K. (2009). The Role of Individual Differences in Job Satisfaction among Indonesians and Malaysians. *European Journal of Social Sciences*, 10(4), 496-511.

Barnard, C. I. (1938). *The Functions of the Executive*. Cambridge, Mass: Harvard University.

Barrett, D.J. (2008). *Leadership Communication* (2nd edition). New York: McGraw Hill-Irwin.

Baughman, J. P. (1964). James Montgomery on Factory Management, 1832. *Business History Review*, Summer, 42(2), 219-226.

Bennis, W., & Nanus, B. (1985). *Leaders: The Strategies for Taking Charge*. New York: Harper and Row.

Bernardin, H.J., & Russell, J.E. (1998). Human Resource Management (2nd edition). San Francisco, CA: McGraw-Hill Companies.

Bernhard, H. B., & Ingols, C. A. (1988). Six Lessons for the Corporate Classroom. *Harvard Business Review*, September-October, 40-46.

Bjork, I.T., Samdal, G.B., Hansen, B.S., Torstad, S. & Hamilton, G.A. (2007). Job Satisfaction in a Norwegian Population of Nurses: A Questionnaire Survey. *International Journal of Nursing Studies*, 44, 747-757.

Bolino, M.C., & Turnley, W.H. (2003). Going the Extra Mile: Cultivating and Managing Employee Citizenship Behavior. *Academy of Management Executive*, 17(3), 60-71.

Bolman, L.G., & Deal, T.E. (2003). *Reframing Organizations: Artistry, Choice, and Leadership* (3rd edition). San Francisco, CA: Jossey Bass.

Bolman, L.G., & Deal, T.E. (2008). *Reframing Organizations: Artistry, Choice, and Leadership* (4th edition). San Francisco, CA: Jossey Bass.

Bott, J., Faulk, D., Guntupalli, A., Devaraj, S., & Holmes, M. (2011). An Examination of Generational Differences and Media Exposure. *The Journal of Applied Management and Entrepreneurship*, 16(4), 78-100.

Bowman, G.W., Jones, L.W., Peterson, R.A., Gronouski, J.A., & Mahoney, R.M. (1964). What Helps or Harms Promotability. *Harvard Business Review*, 42(1), 6-18.

Brewer, E., & Tomlinson, J. W. C. (1964). The Manager's Workday. *Journal of Industrial Economics,* 12, 191-197.

Bryant, A. (2011). Google's Quest to Build a Better Boss. Retrieved on September 8, 2012 from: http://www.nytimes.com/2011/03/13/business/13hire.html?pagewanted=all&_moc.semityn.www

Burns, J.M. (1978). *Leadership*. New York: Harper Row.

Burns, T., & Stalker, G. M. (1961). *The Management of Innovation*. London: Tavistock Publications.

Cable, D.M., & Edwards, J.R. (2004). Complementary and Supplementary Fit: A Theoretical and Empirical Investigation. *Journal of Applied Psychology*, 89, 822-834.

Carlson, S. (1951). *Executive Behavior*. Stockholm: Stromborgs.

Carroll, S. J., & Gillen, D. J. (1987). Are the Classical Management Functions Useful in Describing Managerial Work? *Academy of Management Review*, 12(1), 38-51.

Carson, P.P., Lanier, P.A., Carson, K.D., & Guidry, B.N. (2000). Clearing a Path Through the Management Fashion Jungle: Some Preliminary Trailblazing. *Academy of Management Journal*, 43(6), 1143-1158.

Casserly, M. (2012). The Real Origins of the Gender Pay Gap— And How We Can Turn it Around. Retrieved on September 3, 2012 from: http://www.forbes.com/sites/meghancasserly/2012/07/05/real-origins-gender-pay-gap-how-we-can-turn-it-around/

Coleman, V.I., & Broman, W.C. (2000). Investigating the Underlying Structure of the Citizenship Performance Domain. *Human Resource Management Review*, 10, 25-44.

Colquitt, J.A., Lepine, J.A., & Wesson, M.J. (2011). *Organizational Behavior* (2nd edition). New York: McGraw-Hill.

Crainer, S. (2000). *The Management Century: A Critical Review of 20th Century Thought and Practice*. San Francisco, CA: Josey-Bass Publishers.

Darwin, C. (1872/1965). *The Expression of the Emotions in Man and Animals*. Chicago:
University of Chicago Press.

Davies, J., & Easterby-Smith, M. (1984). Learning and Developing from Managerial Work Experiences. *Journal of Management Studies*, 21(2), 169-183.

De Geus, A. (1997). *The Living Company*. Harvard Business School Publishing.

Delong, T. J. (1982). Reexamining the Career Anchor Model. *Personnel*, May-June, 50-61.

Denning, S. (2012). Apple's Employees Have a Hell of a Ride. Retrieved on September 18, 2012 from: http://www.forbes.com/sites/stevedenning/2012/06/25/apples-employees-have-a-hell-of-a-ride/

De Meyer, A., Loch, C. H., & Pich, M. T. (2002). Managing Project Uncertainty: From Variation to Chaos. *MIT Sloan Management Review*, 43(2), 60-67.

Dess, G.G., Rshee, A., McLaughlin, K.J., & Priem, R.L. (1995). The New Corporate Architecture. *Academy of Management Executive*, 9(3), 7-20.

Dill, R. D., Hilton, T. L., & Reitman, W. R. (1964). *The New Managers: Patterns of Behavior and Development*. Englewood Cliffs, NJ: Prentice Hall, Inc.

Dols, J., Landrum, P., & Wieck, K. (2010). Leading and Managing an Intergenerational Workforce. *Creative Nursing*, 16(2), 68-74.

Drucker, P.F. (1955). *The Practice of Management*. New York: The Free Press.

Drucker, P.F. (1994). The Age of Social Transformation. *The Atlantic Monthly*, 274, 53-80.

Drucker, P.F. (1999). *Management Challenges for the 21st Century*. New York: Harper Collins Publishers, Inc.

DuBrin, A.J. (2007). *Human Relations: Interpersonal Job-Oriented Skills* (9th edition). Upper Saddle River, NJ: Pearson Publishers.

Earley, P.C., & Mosakowski, E. (2004). Cultural Intelligence. *Harvard Business Review*, 82(10), October, 139-153.

Edmondson, G. (2006). BMW's Dream Factory. *BusinessWeek*, 70-80.

Emeagwali, S.N. (2011). Millennials: Leading the Charge for Change. *Techniques*, 23-26.

Esposito, F., Garman, S., Hickman, J., Watson, N., & Wheat, A. (2002). America's 50 Best Companies for Minorities. *Fortune*, 122-128.

Farag, A. A., McGuinness, S. T., & Anthony, M. K. (2009). Nurses' Perception of their Manager's Leadership Style and Unit Climate: Are there Generational Differences. *Journal of Nursing Management, 26*, 26-24.

Farnham, A. (1997). The Man Who Changed Work Forever. *Fortune*, 100-115.

Fayol, H. (1930). *Industrial and General Administration.* J. A. Coubrough. Geneva: International Management Institute.

Feurer, D. (1988). Making the Leap. *Training,* 25(12), 63-68.

Fiedler, F. E. (1960). *The Leader's Psychological Distance and Group Effectiveness.* In D. Cartwright and A. Zander (Eds.), Group dynamics: Research and theory (2nd edition).

Fisher, A. (2005). Holding on to Global Talent. *BusinessWeek.* Retrieved on April 7, 2012 from: http://money.cnn.com/magazines/fortune/fortune_archiv e/2005/10/31/8359141/index.htm

Folger, R., & Skarlicki, D. P. (1998). When Tough Times Make Tough Bosses: Managerial Distancing as a Function of Layoff Blame. *Academy of Management Journal,* 41(1), 79-87.

Fong, R.S., Vogel, R.E., & Bunetello, S. (1995). Blood-In, Blood-Out: The Rationale Behind Defecting from Prison Gangs. *Journal of Gang Research,* 2(4), 45-51.

Freiberg, K., & Freiberg, J. (1998). *Nuts: Southwest Crazy Recipe for Business and Personal Success.* New York, NY: Broadway.

Friedman, T.L. (2006). *The World is Flat. A Brief History of the Twenty-First Century.* New York: Farrar, Straus, and Giroux.

French, J., & Raven, B. H. (1959). The Bases of Social Power. In D. Cartwright (Ed.), Studies in social power (pp. 150-167). Ann Arbor, MI: Institute for Social Research.

Galbraith, J. R. (1980). *Applying* Theory to the Management of Organizations. In W. M. Evan (Ed.), Frontiers in organization and management, 151-167. New York: Praeger.

Gentry, W. A., Deal, J. J., Griggs, T. L., Mondore, S. P., & Cox, B. D. (2011). A Comparison of Generational Differences in Endorsement of Leadership Practices with Actual Leadership Skill Level. *Consulting Psychology Journal: Practice & Research*, 63(1), 39-49.

Gibson, J. W., & Tesone, D. V. (2001). Management Fads: Emergence, Evolution, and Implications for Managers. *Academy of Management Executive*, 15(4), 122-133.

Gibson, J.W., Greenwood, R. A., Murphy, E. F. (2010). Analyzing Generational Values Among Managers and Non-Managers for Sustainable Organizational Effectiveness. *SAM Advanced Management Journal*, 75(1), 33-43.

Goleman, D. (1996). *Emotional Intelligence: Why it Can Matter More Than IQ*. London: Bloomsbury Publishing.

Goleman, D. (1999). *Working with Emotional Intelligence*. London: Bloomsbury Publishing.

Green, H. (2009). How Amazon Aims to Keep You Clicking. *BusinessWeek*, March 2, 2009, pp. 34-40.

Greenleaf, R.K. (1970). *The Servant as Leader*. Indianapolis: The Robert Greenleaf Center.

Griffeth, R.W., Gaertner, S., & Sager, J.K. (1999). Taxonomic Model of Withdrawal Behaviors: The Adaptive Response Model. *Human Resources Management Review*, 9, 577-590.

Grusky, D. (1966). Career Mobility and Organizational Commitment. *Administrative Science Quarterly*, 10, 488-503.

Hall, D. T. (1986). Dilemmas in Linking Succession Planning to Individual Executive Learning. *Human Resource Management*, Summer, 25(2), 235-265.

Hall, D. T. (1989). How Top Management and the Organization Itself Can Block Effective Executive Succession. *Human Resource Management*, Spring, 28(1), 5-24.

Hallowell, E.M. (2011). *Shine: Using Brain Science to Get the Best From Your People*. Boston, MA: Harvard Business Review.

Hamper, B. (1991). *Rivethead: Tales From the Assembly Line*. New York: Warner Books, Inc.

Hartman, J. H., & McCambridge, J. (2011), Optimizing Millenials' Communication Styles. *Business Communication Quarterly*, 74(1), 22-44.

Hays, R. D. (1985). The Myth and Reality of Supervisory Development. *Business Horizons*, January-February, 75-79.

Herda, E. (1999). *Research Conversations and Narrative: A Critical Hermeneutic Orientation in Participatory Inquiry*. Westport, CT: Praeger Publishers.

Herman, M. L., & Oliver, B. B. (2002). A Primer for Crisis Management. *Risk Management*, 49(1), 43-48.

Hersey, P., & Blanchard, K.H. (1969). Life-Cycle-Theory of Leadership. *Training and Development Journal*, 23, 26-34.

Herzberg, F., Mausner, B. & Snyderman, B.B. (1959). *The Motivation to Work*. New York: John Wiley.

Hewlett, S. A, Sherbin, L., & Sumberg, K. (2009). How Generation Y and Baby Boomers Will Reshape Your Agenda. *Harvard Business Review*, July-August, 71-77.

Higgins, J.M., & McAllaster, C. (2004). If You Want Strategic Change, Don't Forget to Change Your Cultural Artifacts. *Journal of Change Management*, 4, 63-74.

Hill, L. A. (1992). *Becoming a Manager: Mastery of a New Identity*. Boston, Massachusetts: Harvard Business School Press.

Hirsch, M., & Keith, H. E. (1997). The Unraveling of Japan Inc. *Foreign Affairs*, 76(2), 11-16.

Hodgetts, R. M., Kuratko, D. F., & Hornsby, J. S. (1999). Quality Implementation in Small Business: Perspectives from Baldridge Award Winners. *S.A.M. Advanced Management Journal*, 64(1), 37-47.

Hom, P.W., Katerburg, R., & Hulin, C.L. (1979). Comparative Examination of Three Approaches to the Predication of Turnover. *Journal of Applied Psychology*, 64, 280-290.

Howe, N., & Strauss, W. (2007). *Millennials & K-12 Schools: Educational Strategies for a New Generation*. Great Falls, VA: LifeCourse Associates.

Hrebiniak, L. G., & Alutto, J. A. (1972). Personal and Role Related Factors in the Development of Organizational Commitment. *Administrative Science Quarterly*, 17, 555-573.

Jackofsky, E.F., & Peters, L.H. (1983). Job Turnover Versus Company Turnover: Reassessment of the March and Simon Participation Hypothesis. *Journal of Applied Psychology*, 68, 490-495.

Jeffrey, S.A. (2009). Justifiability and the Motivational Power of Tangible Noncash Iincentives. *Human Performance*, 22, 143-155.

Johnson, A. L., & Luthans, F. (1990). The Relationship Between Leadership and Management: An Empirical Assessment. *Journal of Managerial Studies*, 2(1), 13-25.

Johnson, R. A., Neelankavil, J. P., & Jadhav, A. (1986). Developing the Executive Resource. *Business Horizons*, November-December, 29-33.

Jones, G. R. (1986). Socialization Tactics, Self-Efficacy, and Newcomers' Adjustments to Organizations. *Academy of Management Journal*, 29(2), 262-279.

Jones, G.R. & George, J.M. (2008). *Contemporary Management*. New York: McGraw-Hill.

Kaifi, B.A., & Medenhall, S. (2012). Strategic Leadership Applied to Retail Management: Joe Contrucci Discusses the 21st Century Dynamic Workforce. *Journal of Applied Management and Entrepreneurship*, 17(4), 103-108.

Kaifi, B.A., & Do, Q. (2012). Critical Concepts Applied to Leadership in Energy and Environmental Design: Insights from Karen Maggio. *Journal of Applied Management and Entrepreneurship*, 17(2), 97-103.

Kaifi, B.A., & Noori, S.A. (2011). Organizational Behavior: A Study on Managers, Employees, and Teams. *Journal of Management Policy and Practice*, 12(1), 88- 97.

Kaifi, B.A. (2010). *Understanding Organizational Behavior.* Presentation at Carrington College California on July 6, 2010 from 9:15AM to 10:00AM and also 11:30AM- 12:15PM.

Kaifi, B.A. (2010). *Managing Your Future: An Educational Guide.* Davie, Florida: ILEAD Academy.

Kaifi, B.A. (2009). *21ˢᵗ Century Leadership in Healthcare.* Pages 90-100. Chapter Twelve in the Pharmaceutical Technician Laboratory Manual by Sandeep Bansal. Jones and Bartlett Publications, Boston: Massachusetts.

Kane, S. (2012). *Generation X.* Retrieved on September 2, 2012 from: http://legalcareers.about.com/od/practicetips/a/Generation X.htm

Kanter, R. M. (1989). The New Managerial Work. *Harvard Business Review,* November-December, 85-91.

Katz, D., & Kahn, R. L. (1978). *The Social Psychology of Organizations* (2ⁿᵈ ed.) New York: John Wiley and Sons.

Kimberly, J. R. (1981). *Managerial Innovation.* In P. C. Nystrom and W. H. Starbuck (Eds.), Handbook of organizational design, 84-104. New York: Oxford University Press.

Koretz, G. (2003). Hate Your Job? Join the Club. *BusinessWeek,* October 6, 2003, p. 40.

Kouzes, J.M., & Posner, B.Z. (2003). *Encouraging the Heart.* San Francisco, CA: Jossey Bass.

Kovach, B. E. (1986). The Derailment of Fast-Track Managers. *Organizational Dynamics,* Autumn, 41-48.

Kovach, K. (1999). *Employee Motivation: Addressing a Crucial Factor in Your Organization's Performance. Human Resource Development.* Ann Arbor, MI: University of Michigan Press.

Lamberton, L.H., & Minor, L. (2010). *Human Relations: Strategies for Success* (4th ed.). Burr Ridge, IL: McGraw-Hill.

Lantz, P. (2008). Gender and Leadership in Healthcare Administration: 21st Century Progress and Challenges. *Journal of Healthcare Management,* 53(5), 291-301.

Leavitt, H.J. (1965). *Applied Organizational Change in Industry: Structural, Technological, and Humanistic Approaches.* In J.G. March, ed., Handbook of Organizations. Chicago: Rand McNally, 1144-1170.

Levering, R., & Moskowitz, M. (1993). *The 100 Best Companies to Work for in America.* New York, NY: Plume.

Levering, R.,& Moskowitz, M. (2009). *100 Best Companies to Work for.* Fortune, February 2, 2009. Retrieved on September 30, 2012 from: http://money.cnn.com/magazines/fortune/bestcompanies /2009/snapshots/1.html

Levinson, D. J. (1978). *Seasons of a Man's Life.* New York: Knopf.

Levinson, H. (1965). Who is to Blame for the Maladaptive Manager? *Harvard Business Review,* November-December, 143-158.

Lewin, K., Lippitt, R., & White, R.K. (1939). Patterns of Aggressive Behavior in Experimentally Created Social Climates. *Journal of Social Psychology,* 10, 271-299.

Locke, E.A. (1976). *The Nature and Causes of Job Satisfaction.* In Handbook of Industrial and Organizational Psychology, (Ed.) M. Dunnette. Chicago, IL: Rand McNally, 1297-1349.

Locke, E.A., & Latham, G.P. (1990). *A Theory of Goal Setting and Task Performance.* NJ: Prentice Hall.

Lorsch, J. W., & Mathias, P. F. (1987). When Professionals Have to Manage. *Harvard Business Review,* July-August, 78-83.

Louis, M. R. (1980). Surprise and Sense-Making: What Newcomers Experience in Entering Unfamiliar Organization Settings. *Administrative Science Quarterly,* 25, June, 226-250.

Louis, M. R. (1982). Managing Career Transition: A Missing Link in Career Development. *Organizational Dynamics,* Spring, 68-77.

Luft, J., & Ingham, H. (1955). *The Johari Window: A Graphic Model of Interpersonal Awareness.* Proceedings of the Western Training Laboratory in Group Development (Los Angeles: UCLA).

Luthans, F., Rosenkrantz, S. A., & Hennessey, H. W. (1985). What Do Successful Managers Really Do? An Observation Study of Managerial Activities. *The Journal of Applied Behavioral Science,* 21(3), 255-270.

Lumsden, G., Lumsden, D., & Wiethoff, C. (2010). *Communicating In Groups and Teams: Sharing leadership* (5th ed). Boston, MA: Wadsworth Cengage.

Maslow, A.H. (1943). A Theory of Human Motivation. *Psychological Review,* 50, 370-396.

Mathieu, J. E., & Zajac, D. M. (1990). A Review and Meta-Analysis of the Antecedents, Correlates, and Consequences of Organizational Commitment. *Journal of Applied Psychology*, 108, 171-194.

Mathis, R.L., & Jackson, J.H. (1994). *Human Resource Management* (7th ed.). San Francisco, CA: West Publishing Corporation.

Maxwell, J.C. (2010). *Everyone Communicates Few Connect: What the Most Effective People Do Differently*. Nashville, TN: Thomas Nelson Publishing.

McCall, M. W. Jr., & Lombardo, M. M. (1983). *Off The Track: Why and How Successful Executives Get Derailed*. Center for Creative Leadership, Report 21, Greensboro, North Carolina.

McClelland, D.C. (1961). *The Achieving Society*. Princeton, NJ: D. Van Nostrand.

McCoy, S.P., & Aamodt, M.G. (2010). A Comparison of Law Enforcement Divorce Rates With Those of Other Occupations. *Journal of Police and Criminal Psychology*, 25(1), 1-16.

McGee-Cooper, A., Trammell, D., & Looper, G. (2008). The Power of LUV: An Inside Peek at the Innovative Culture Committee of Southwest Airlines. *Reflections: The SoL Journal*, 9(1), 49-54.

McGregor, D. (1960). *The Human Side of Enterprise*. New York: McGraw-Hill.

McKnight, D.H., Phillips, B., & Hardgrave, B.C. (2009). Which Reduces IT Turnover Intention the Worst: Workplace Characteristics or Job Characteristics? *Information and Management*, 46, 167-174.

McNerney, D.J. (1996). Creating a Motivated Workforce. *HR Focus*, August.

Mintzberg, H. (1973). *The Nature of Managerial Work*. New York, NY: Harper and Row.

Mintzberg, H. (1975). The Manager's Job: Folklore or Fact? *Harvard Business Review*, 53(4), 49-61.

Mintzberg, H. (1996). Ten Ideas Designed to Rile Everyone Who Cares About Management. *Harvard Business Review*, July-August, 61-67.

Morrison, A., & Glinow, M. (1995). *Women and Minorities in Management*. In The Leader's Companion by J. Thomas Wren, pp. 168-181. NY: The Free Press.

Motowidlo, S.J. (2000). Some Basic Issues Related to Contextual Performance and Organizational Citizenship Behavior in Human Resource Management. *Human Resource Management Review*, 10, 115-126.

Mujtaba, B.G. (2008). Task and Relationship Orientation of Thai and American Business Students Based on Cultural Contexts. *Research in Higher Education Journal*, 1(1), 38-57.

Mujtaba, B.G., Khanfar, N.M., & Khanfar, S.M. (2010). Leadership Tendencies of Government Employees in Oman: A Study of Task and Relationship Based on Age and Gender. *Public Organization Review: A Global Journal*, 10, 173-190.

Mujtaba, B.G. (2010). *Workforce Diversity Management: Challenges, Competencies, and Strategies* (2nd ed.). Davie, FL: ILEAD Academy.

Mujtaba, B.G., & Kaifi, B.A. (2010). An Inquiry Into Eastern Leadership Orientation of Working Adults in Afghanistan. *Journal of Leadership Studies*, 4(1), 36-46.

Mujtaba, B.G., & Kaifi, B.A. (2010). Afghan-Americans' Awareness of Business Ethics: A Study Based on Gender, Age, and Education. *Business & Professional Ethics Journal*, 29(1-4), 33-61.

Mujtaba, B.G., & McCartney, T. (2007). *Managing Workplace Stress and Conflict Amid Change*. Coral Springs, FL: Llumina Press.

Mumford, A. (1987). Helping Managers Learn to Learn. *Journal of Management Development*, 6(5), 49-60.

Murphy, A., & Janeke, H. C. (2009). The Relationship Between Thinking Styles and Emotional Intelligence: An Exploratory Study. *South African Journal of Psychology*, 39(3), 357-375.

Myers, M. S. (1966). Conditions for Manager Motivation. *Harvard Business Review*, January-February, 58-71.

Nelson, D.L., & Quick, J.C. (2011). *Organizational Behavior* (7th ed.). Mason, OH: Cengage Learning.

Northouse, P. G. (2004). *Leadership: Theory and Practice* (3rd ed.). Thousand Oaks, California: SAGE.

Ohlott, P. J., Ruderman, M. N., & McCauley, C. D. (1994). Gender Differences in Managers' Developmental Job Experiences. *Academy of Management Journal*, 37(1), 46-67.

O'Reilly, C. A., Chatman, J. A., & Caldwell, D. F. (1991). People and Organizational Culture: A Profile Comparison

Approach to Person-Organization Fit. *Academy of Management Journal*, 34, 487-516.

O'Toole, J. (1995). *Leading Change: Overcoming the Ideology of Comfort and the Tyranny of Custom*. San Francisco, CA: Jossey Bass.

Ouchi, W.G. (1981). *Theory Z: How American Business Can Meet the Japanese Challenge*. Reading, MA: Addison-Wesley.

Parker, L. D. (1984). Control in Organizational Life: The Contribution of Mary Parker Follet. *Academy of Management Review*, 9, 741-754.

Pearce, J. L. (1998). *Volunteers—The Organizational Behavior of Unpaid Workers*. London: Walter De Gruyter and Company.

Perls, F., Hefferline, R., & Goodman, P. (1988). *Gestalt Therapy*. New York: Random House.

Peters, L.H., Bhagat, R.S., & O'Connor, E.J. (1981). An Examination of the Independent and Joint Contributions of Organizational Commitment and Job Satisfaction on Employee Intentions to Quit. *Group and Organization Studies*, 6, 77-83.

Peters, T. (1988). *Thriving on Chaos: Handbook for Management Revolution*. New York, NY: HarperCollins Publishers.

Pfeffer, J. & Veiga, J.F. (1999). Putting People First for Organizational Success. *Academy of Management Executive*, 13(2), 37-48.

Phillips, J. J. (1986). Corporate Boot Camp for Newly Appointed Supervisors. *Personnel Journal*, January, 70-74.

Phillips, J. S., & Lord, R. G. (1980, April). Determinants of Intrinsic Motivation: Locus of Control and Competence Information as Components of Deci's Cognitive Evaluation Theory. *Journal of Applied Psychology*, 65(2), 211-225.

Podsakoff, N.P., Whiting, S.W., Podsakoff, P.M., & Blume, B.D. (2009). Individual –and Organizational Level Consequences of Organizational Citizenship Behaviors: A Meta-Analysis. *Journal of Applied Psychology*, 94, 122-141.

Podsakoff, P.M., Ahearne, M., & MacKenzie, S.B. (1997). Organizational Citizenship Behavior and the Quantity and Quality of Work Group Performance. *Journal of Applied Psychology*, 82, 262-270.

Portillo, S., & Dehart-Davis, L. (2009). Gender and Organizational Rule Abidance. Public *Administration Review*, 69(2), 339-347.

Pounder, J. (2008). Transformational Leadership: Practicing What We Teach in the Management Classroom. *Journal of Education for Business*, 84(1), 2-6.

Raelin, J. A. (1989). An Anatomy of Autonomy: Managing Professionals. *The Academy of Management Executive*, 3(3), 216-228.

Rainey, H.G. (2003). *Understanding and Managing Public Organizations* (3rd ed.). San Francisco: Jossey-Bass.

Rao, P. (2006). Emotional Intelligence: The Sine Qua Non for a Clinical Leadership Toolbox. *Journal of Communication Disorders*, 39(4), 310-319.

Rath, T., & Conchie, B. (2009). Strengths Based Leadership. NY: Gallup Press.

Reeves, T. C., Duncan, W. J., & Ginter, P. M. (2001). Motion Study in Management and the Arts: A historical Example. *Journal of Management Inquiry*, 10(2), 137-149.

Rindfuss, R. R., Cooksey, E. C., & Sutterlin, R. L. (1999). Young Adult Occupational Achievement: Early Expectations Versus Behavioral Reality. *Work and Occupations*, 26 (2), 220-263.

Robbins, S.P., & Coulter, M.C. (2005). *Management* (8th ed). Upper Saddle River, NJ: Pearson.

Robbins, S.P., & DeCenzo, D.A. (2007). *Supervision Today* (5th ed.). Upper Saddle River, NJ: Pearson Prentice Hall.

Roberts, M. (2007). Southwest CEO's 2006 Less Than $1M. *Forbes.com*, March 30, 2007.

Rosenberg, M. (2009). *Baby Boom: The Population Baby Boom of 1946-1964 in the United States*. Retrieved on September 2, 2012 from: http://geography.about.com/od/populationgeography/a/babyboom.htm

Salami, S. (2010). Conflict Resolution Strategies and Organizational Citizenship Behavior: The Moderating Role of Trait Emotional Intelligence. *Social Behavior and Personality*, 38(1), 75-86.

Salahuddin, M. M. (2010). Generational Differences Impact on Leadership Style and Organizational Success. *Journal of Diversity Management*, 5(2), 1-6.

Salovey, P., & Mayer, J. D. (1990). *Emotional Intelligence: Imagination, Cognition, and Personality*. New York: Harper.

Samuel, S. (1996). Mary Parker Follett--Prophet of Management: A Celebration of Writings From the 1920s. *Academy of Management Review*, 21(3), 863-867.

Schein, E. H. (1967). Attitude Change During Management Education. *Administrative Science Quarterly*, 11, 601-628.

Schein, E. H. (1975). *Career Dynamics: Matching Individual and Organizational Needs*. New York: Addison-Wesley.

Schein, E. H. (1975). How "Career Anchors" Hold Executives to Their Career Paths. *Personnel*, May-June, 11-24.

Schein, E.H. (1985). *Organizational Culture and Leadership: A Dynamic View*. San Francisco, CA: Jossey Bass.

Schneider, B., Goldstein, H.W., & Smith, D.B. (1995). The ASA Framework: An Update. *Personnel Psychology*, 48, 747-773.

Schwartz, T., Jones, J., & McCarty, C. (2010). *The Way We're Working Isn't Working*. New York, NY: Free Press.

Senge, P. (1990). *The Fifth Discipline*. New York: Doubleday.

Shambaugh, D. (1991). The Soldier and the State in China: The Political Work System in the People's Liberation Army. *Chinese Quarterly*, 127, 527-568.

Simons, N. (2010). Leveraging Generational Work Styles to Meet Business Objectives. *Information Management*, 44(1), 28-33

Silverthorne, C., & Wang, T. (2001). Situational Leadership Style as a Predictor of Success and Productivity Among Taiwanese Business Organizations. *The Journal of Psychology*, 135(4), 399-412.

Simon, H. A. (1987). Making Management Decisions: The Role of Intuition and Emotion. *Academy of Management Executive*, February, 57-64.

Skinner, B.F. (1938). *The Behavior of Organisms. An Experimental Analysis*. New York: Appleton-Century-Crofts.

Skinner, W., & Sasser, W. E. (1997). Managers With Impact: Versatile and Inconsistent. *Harvard Business Review*, November-December, 140-148.

Smith, A. (1776). *An Inquiry Into the Nature and Cause of the Wealth of Nations*. Philadelphia: Congressional Reports.

Snell, R. S. (1987). Turning Bad Times Into Good Times and Good Times Into Better Ones. *Group Relations Training Association Bulletin*, Winter, 15-19.

Snell, R. S. (1988). The Emotional Cost of Managerial Learning at Work. *Management Education and Development*, 19(4), 332-340.

Spector, R., & McCarthy, D. (1995). *The Nordstrom Way: The Inside Story of America's #1 Customer Service Company*. New York: Wiley.

Stephens, G. K., & Sommer, S. M. (2001). Lyman Porter: A Celebration of Excellence in Mentoring. *Journal of Management Inquiry*, 10(2), 190-196.

Stogdill, R.M. (1974). *Handbook of Leadership: A Survey of Theory and Research*. New York: Free Press.

Strickland, O. J., & Galimba, M. (2001). Managing Time: The Effects of Personal Goal Setting on Resource Allocation Strategy and Task Performance. *The Journal of Psychology*, 135 (4), 357-367.

Tajaddini, R., & Mujtaba, B.G. (2009). Stress Perceptions and Leadership Orientation of Malaysians: Exploring Their Similarities and Difference with Americans. *Chinese Business Review*, 8(8), 26-42.

Taylor, F. W. (1903). *Shop Management*. New York: Harper and Row.

Taylor, F. W. (1911). *The Principles of Scientific Management*. New York: Harper Brothers.

Tolbzie, A. (2008). Generational Differences in the Workplace. *Research and Training Center of Community Living*, 19, 1-13.

Tompkins, T. C. (2001). Using Advocacy and Inquiry to Improve the Thinking Process of Future Managers. *The Journal of Management Education*, 25(5), 553-571.

Tuckman, B.W. (1965). Developmental Sequence in Small Groups. *Psychological Bulletin*, 63, 384-499.

Van de Ven, A. (2000). The Practice of Management Knowledge. *The Academy of Management News*, 31(3), 4-5.

Vargish, T. (1991). The Value of Humanities in Executive Development. *Sloan Management Review*, Spring, 83-91.

Verschoor, C. C. (2002). Were Enron's Ethical Missteps a Major Cause of its Downfall? *Strategic Finance*, 83(8), 22-25.

Vroom, V. (1973). A New Look at Managerial Decision Making. *Organizational Dynamics*, 73(1), 66-80.

Wahn, J. C. (1998). Sex Differences in the Continuance Component of Organizational Commitment. *Group & Organization Management*, 23(3), 256-266.

Weber, G. (2005). Preserving the Counter Culture. *Workforce Management*, 84, 28–34.

Welch, J.F. (2001). *Jack: Straight From the Gut*. New York: Warner Books Inc.

Winston, B. E., & Patterson, K. (2006). An Integrative Definition of Leadership. *International Journal of Leadership Studies*, 1(2), 6-66.

Woods, M., & Dorset, S. (1988). *The New Manager: A Guide to Improving the Skills of People Management for Newly Appointed Managers*. New Jersey: Element Books.

Wrege, C.D., & Hodgetts, R.M. (2000). Frederick W. Taylor's 1899 Pig Iron Observations: Examining Fact, Fiction, and Lessons for the New Millennium. *Academy of Management Journal*, 43(6), 1283-1291.

Wren, D. A. (1992). The Nature of Managerial Work: A Comparison of Real Managers and Traditional Management. *Journal of Managerial Issues*, 4(1), 17-30.

Wren, D. A. (1994). *The Evolution of Management Thought* (4th ed.). New York: John Wiley and Sons, Inc.

Wyld, D. (2008). How Do Women Fare When the Promotion Rules Change? *Academy of Management Perspectives*, 22(4), 83-85.

Xenikou, A., & Simosi, M. (2006). Organizational Culture and Transformational Leadership as Predictors of Business Unit Performance. *Journal of Managerial Psychology*, 21(6), 566-579.

ABOUT THE AUTHOR

Dr. Belal A. Kaifi completed a Post-Doctoral Program in Business Administration with an emphasis in Management and Marketing at the University of Florida. He is academically qualified (AACSB-AQ) to teach in the departments of Business Administration and Education. Dr. Kaifi completed his Doctoral degree in Organization and Leadership at the University of San Francisco. He earned a Master's degree in Public Administration with an emphasis in Human Resource Management and a second Master's degree in Business Administration. His undergraduate degree is in Business Administration with an emphasis in Management. Dr. Kaifi has over ten years of combined experience in academia, including teaching at the undergraduate and graduate levels (both traditional classrooms and online), managing an educational department, consulting, and researching. Dr. Kaifi has published over 30 peer-reviewed articles since 2008. This is Dr. Kaifi's third book, having previously published the following books:

- **Managing Your Future: An Educational Guide (2010)**
- **The Impact of 9/11 on Afghan-American Leaders (2009)**

Dr. Kaifi has extensive experience with cross-cultural management, budget planning and administration, training and succession planning, curriculum design and development, accreditation planning, management development, performance evaluations, leadership training and development, online education, faculty recruitment, program review, student learning outcome (SLO) assessment, and AACSB assurance of learning

(AOL) standards. Furthermore, Dr. Kaifi has sat on numerous educational advisory committees and faculty councils as well as offered his expertise as a mentor to many younger, less experienced professors over the years.

In addition, during his academic career, Dr. Kaifi has had the opportunity to teach the following undergraduate and graduate level courses:

- Organizational Behavior
- Organizational Change
- Staffing, Performance Management, and Training
- Leadership in Action: Organizational Teams
- Human Relations and Organizational Behavior
- Organization Theory
- Organizational Behavior and Management
- Management Communication
- International Business
- Managing and Leading Contemporary Organizations
- Business Communication
- Personnel and Human Resources Management
- Organizational Behavior and Teamwork
- Contemporary Business Research Methodology
- Capstone in General Management
- Hospitality Marketing
- Global Issues

In his spare time, Dr. Kaifi enjoys traveling. Thus far, he has traveled to Afghanistan, Sweden, Germany, Mexico, Canada, and Dubai. He considers himself a global citizen.

INDEX

"Be the change you wish to see in the world."

~ Mahatma Gandhi

Appendix

A General Framework for a Research Proposal

Section	Description	Length
Problem	This section contains a fairly detailed description of the research problem to be studied. The following should also be addressed in this section: What is the motivation for the study? What is the problem? Why is the problem important? What new knowledge will your research bring to the field?	**This section should be approx. 2 to 4 pages.**
Objectives	In this section, the research objectives should be clearly stated.	**This section should be approx. 1 to 3 pages.**
Literature Review	Related research studies should be reviewed, including related literature surveys, if there are any. This section should have at least 10-25 different references (journal articles and books only—no Websites).	**This section should be approx. 4 to 7 pages.**
Hypotheses	What are the hypotheses to be tested? You should have 3-5 hypotheses.	**This section should be approx. 1 to 2 pages.**

Methodology	What is (are) the suggested methodology (methodologies) for tackling the research problem. These may include: - Statistical analysis (Quantitative) - Structured interviews (Qualitative) What are the limitations of the study? These may include assumptions about the environment, population, and/or scope. - How will these assumptions be justified?	**This section should be approx. 2 to 4 pages.**
Data Collection	How will you collect your data? What specific data will be needed for the study? Do you need to create a survey? Will you need to travel? Give details of this entire process.	**This section should be approx. 1 to 3 pages.**
Validation	Since this is only a proposal, this section is not needed.	N/A
Results and Conclusions	Since this is only a proposal, this section is not needed.	N/A

9 781625 506085